P9-CMS-822

CROSS STITCH
SILHOUETTES

CROSS STITCH SILHOUETTES

ADELE WELSBY

David & Charles

PICTURE ON PAGE 2

Watery motifs taken from the Childhood Classics chapter feature on these three projects. The use of variegated threads adds a contemporary dimension to the silhouette work. The bewitching mermaid on the small cupboard was stitched on forget-me-not blue 28 count Jobelin with two shades of Bravo variegated thread – A91 for the body flesh tones and A115 for the rest of the design. The design was mounted onto card, glued to the front of a ready-made cupboard and the beading which holds the card in place was painted. A money-box (available from Framecraft) features Noah's Ark stitched on cream 18 count Aida using two strands of A102 Bravo variegated thread. A coat of tinted varnish was applied to the box to match the thread. Seaside holidays are always a favourite and an essential sun hat has a blue lighthouse stitched on cream 28 count Jobelin slipstitched onto the central panel

PICTURE OPPOSITE

Using charts from the Favourite Pastimes chapter, this picture shows a detail of various kitchen motifs stitched in two strands of Delft blue stranded cotton over two threads of 28 count cream Jobelan fabric. The design could be mounted into a wooden tray with brass handles from Framecraft (see Suppliers page 127)

A DAVID & CHARLES BOOK

First published in the UK in 2000
Text and designs Copyright © Adele Welsby 2000
Photography and layout Copyright © David & Charles 2000

ISBN 0 7153 0991 9
Photography by David Johnson
Styling by Kit Johnson
Book design by Diana Knapp
Printed in Italy by Milanostampa SpA
for David & Charles
Brunel House   Newton Abbot   Devon

CONTENTS

INTRODUCTION

THE TECHNIQUE OF SILHOUETTING is an ancient one. Silhouettes or profiles – outlines filled in with flat colour – date from as far back as the Stone Age, when murals depicting the various aspects of the natural world were painted on the walls of limestone caves in France and Spain. The Greeks and Etruscans used profile drawings on their pottery and in religious art and further examples can be seen on fine Minoan frescoes found on Thera. Hieroglyphs were characters used for writing by both the ancient Egyptians and the Aegean civilisations. They were profiles depicting objects, letters or sounds, examples of which were men in short tunics, children in shifts, houses like pagodas, as well as the bow, the arrow, the ship and the bird of prey.

During the seventeenth century shadow portraits were popular. The subject's shadow was cast onto a wall either by candle or lamplight and the silhouetted image was painted onto various materials such as vellum, wax or plaster and then elaborately framed.

With the eighteenth century came the invention of paper and scissors and the art of paper cutting. During this period the infamous French finance minister Etienne de Silhouette (1709–67) tried to introduce harsh financial restrictions on the Royal family and his name became contemptuously associated with his hobby, the art of paper cutting, which was considered an inexpensive pursuit.

The Victorians favoured silhouettes and their preference was to produce pictures of family groups, profiles of heads and shoulders and flowers. They were adventurous and inspired by the dressed prints frequently shown in fashion magazines and catalogues. These silhouette figures were cut out and dressed using fabric, which was then cut to shape and glued to the appropriate section of the figure. Lace, feathers, beads or sequins representing the fashion of the period often enhanced the gowns. These beautiful figures had the delightful title of Amelia.

The art of silhouetting became popular in both Europe and America and important collections were formed including the work of Goethe. There were some important silhouette artists including John Miers, August Edouart, the author of fairy tales Hans Christian Anderson and the illustrator Arthur Rackham. The nineteenth century however, saw the advent and rapid development of photography, which ultimately resulted in the demise of the silhouette artist.

The art of silhouetting still has great artistic value, as can be seen by the cross stitch designs in this book, where the principles of silhouette work have been translated into embroidery. This book is full of crisp, witty and charming designs, exuding a freshness that belies their ancient heritage.

The projects shown made up here use charts from the Borders Galore chapter. A cream guest towel from Fabric Flair has been stitched with a Delft-style border using two strands of stranded cotton in a coffee colour. The lovely fragrance of summer may be brought to any room with a herb and dried-flowered sachet. The central panel of the sachet has been stitched with a vertical band of ribbons and edged with a second band on either side using two strands of plum stranded cotton over two threads of 28 count cream linen. A border of Assisi work swans circle an ornate candle. The candle band was stitched with one strand of natural coloured variegated thread over two threads of 32 count cream coloured linen

MATERIALS & TECHNIQUES

THE MATERIALS needed for producing perfect cross stitch silhouettes are simple and inexpensive, while the techniques are straightforward and easy to master. Do read this section as it describes the tools and materials required plus the basic techniques and stitches you will be using.

MATERIALS

FABRICS

There are many wonderful fabrics available today, in a vast array of colours and catering for many levels of ability. Fabrics used for counted cross stitch are all woven so they have the same number of threads or blocks to 1in (2.5cm) both vertically and horizontally. The two main fabric types used are blockweaves such as Aida, and evenweaves such as linen.

BLOCKWEAVE FABRICS

These fabrics, commonly given the general name of Aida, are made of cotton and are woven in blocks making it very easy to count, as one cross stitch is worked over one block. There is a choice in the number of blocks per 1in (2.5cm), 14 being the most commonly used. Aida is suitable for complete novices and comes in larger counts such as 12 and 8 which have 12 and 8 holes per 1in (2.5cm) respectively, making these useful for small children and the visually impaired because touch can also be used to locate position. The dressing table mirror and hair brush on page 12 have been stitched on 18 count Aida, as has the glasses case on page 70.

EVENWEAVE FABRICS

These fabrics are available in a large range of colours and types and are woven so that there is the same number of threads per 1in (2.5cm) vertically and horizontally, allowing the cross stitching to be of equal height and width. Evenweaves come in a wide variety of thread counts, for example, a 28 count fabric has 28 threads to 1in (2.5cm). As stitching on evenweave is usually done over two threads of the fabric, this produces 14 stitches to 1in (2.5cm), therefore a design worked on 28 count evenweave will be the same size as when stitched on 14 count Aida.

Linen is an evenweave fabric made from flax which has a natural slub adding charm to the finished stitching. The apron on page 28 was stitched on 28 count linen, as was the wedding cushion on page 86.

Jobelan is the trade name for a range of colourful 28 count fabrics made from cotton and modal which makes it strong and easy to care for. It is ideal where a practical application is required, for example for bags, sacks and tablecloths. The three projects shown on page 40 of the Favourite Pastimes chapter have been stitched on Jobelan.

Hardanger fabric is between an Aida and a linen, being woven with pairs of thread. The stitching is usually worked over a pair of threads. The hanging Christmas decorations on page 98 have been stitched on a 22 count Hardanger fabric.

WASTE CANVAS

The designs in this book would be perfect for embellishing clothing, particularly baby wear. Try using waste canvas, which allows you to cross stitch on non-evenweave fabrics.

THREADS

There is a vast choice of threads available today and the cross stitch silhouette designs in this book will allow you to experiment with them. Generally there are few specific makes or code numbers given, just the thread type and colour used, as this will enable you to choose your own thread or use the brands you are most comfortable with. The threads predominantly used in the book are described briefly below.

STRANDED COTTON

The most commonly used thread for cross stitching is six-stranded mercerised cotton (floss) which has a lovely silk-like sheen. It is produced by several manufacturers, including DMC, Anchor and Madeira, and comes in a huge range of colours.

The strands in a skein are usually separated before starting to stitch – the number required for stitching depends on the count of the fabric you're stitching on. Generally two strands are used for cross stitch on 14 count fabrics and three strands on a more open weave such as 11 count. For finer work such as 22 count one strand will give adequate coverage.

In the majority of cases the evenweave and Aida fabrics used in this book have been stitched with two strands of stranded cotton over two threads of evenweave or one block of Aida fabric unless otherwise stated in the stitching notes. The backstitching and long stitches use one strand.

FLOWER THREAD

This is a soft-textured smooth thread with a matt finish which can create quite a different look to a design. It is a single, non-divisible thread ideal for fine work and is available from DMC in a good choice of colours.

RAYON THREAD

Rayon thread has a wonderful glossy, silk-like look perfect for highlighting or for producing a three-dimensional effect. It can also be used as a blending filament. The wedding cushion on page 86 uses yellow rayon thread.

BLENDING FILAMENT

Blending filament is a flat, one-ply reflective filament twisted with a plain fibre. It is used in conjunction with stranded cotton to produce shine, lustre and in some cases luminescence. Follow the manufacturer's instructions for use, as it can be tricky to control. The Christmas table mat on page 98 uses Madeira Rainbow Glissen Gloss most effectively.

METALLIC THREADS

Metallic threads are used to add sparkle to a design as can be seen in the Christmas Joy chapter on page 98. There are many varieties available and with experimentation you will find the thickness required for a particular count of fabric. Metallic threads feel different to stitch with and you will have to take more time to ensure that the metallics sit well on the fabric. Metallics tend to damage easily when passing through fabric and to prevent this, it is best to use short lengths of no more than 46cm (18in) at a time. The wizard toy sack on page 54 uses some metallic threads.

VARIEGATED THREADS

A simple design can be transformed by substituting a single-coloured thread with a variegated one. This type of thread is dyed so that the colour gradually changes from pale to dark tones. Some threads are dyed commercially and come from a set range where the colour change repeats along the length. Hand-dyed threads have a random pattern of shades along the length of the thread. Different effects can be produced depending on the way you stitch with the thread. For a random effect work stitches in a small cluster next to each other. When the colour changes, begin a new cluster. Hand-dyed threads will give a slightly mottled appearance. Standard variegated threads, which are cut into shaded lengths, will produce an ombré effect over a larger area. Stitch a few examples using different ways of stitching to find the right effect for your chosen design. The riverside walk picture on page 28 uses variegated threads.

CARON SPACE-DYED THREAD

This is a hand-made thread with beautiful variegated effects. Generally one strand is used when stitching with Caron threads. The dragonflies and iris picture on page 28 uses Wildflower thread to great effect.

NEEDLES

A blunt tapestry needle is usually used for cross stitch. The most common sizes used are 24 for fabrics up to 14 count and size 26 for 16 count and finer fabrics. Be aware that nickel-plated needles will leave a mark on the fabric if left in it for any length of time. It is recommended that you take the needle out when leaving your work or alternately treat yourself to a gold-plated needle which will not tarnish.

SCISSORS

Sharp, fine-pointed embroidery scissors will be needed for cutting threads and a pair of dressmaking scissors for cutting fabric.

HOOPS AND FRAMES

It is a matter of personal preference whether you use a hoop or frame to house your stitching while working. Some feel that the fabric remains taut, making control of tension easier when using a hoop or frame, which may be of assistance to beginners. Others are concerned with the creasing of the fabric and the damage to stitches that may occur. If you use a hoop, bind the edges of the frame with bias binding to prevent slippage and use tissue paper between the frames to prevent damage to the stitching. When you have finished working remove the fabric from the hoop to avoid excessive crease marks.

TECHNIQUES

USING CHARTS

All the projects use counted cross stitch with the design worked from charts, which are computer generated and easy to read. Some designs are outlined in backstitch and some feature basic blackwork, such as the Eiffel Tower on page 85 and the elephant on page 80.

The charts are divided into squares, so that one square on the chart, which contains a symbol, represents one stitch on your fabric. Blank squares on the chart means that there is no stitching in that area. One stitch on the fabric is over either one block of Aida or two threads of an evenweave fabric. A straight black line on the chart indicates a backstitch. A long stitch is shown by a straight coloured line. A French knot is shown by a coloured knot symbol.

CALCULATING DESIGN SIZE

To calculate the size of the design you wish to stitch look at the chart and count the number of stitches horizontally and vertically. Divide each of these numbers by the number of stitches to 1in (2.5cm) on your fabric (i.e., the count) and this will give you the finished design size. You will then need to add an allowance to this for working the design and final mounting.

EXAMPLE

For a chart 96 x 33 stitched squares the calculation below shows how large the cross stitched design would be on various counts of fabric. (Remember that an evenweave fabric is usually stitched over two threads not one block therefore you need to divide the count by two before you start.)

Stitched squares horizontally	÷ Fabric count	= Design width
96	11	= 8¾in approx.
96	14	= 7in approx.
96	18	= 5¼in approx.

Stitched squares vertically	÷ Fabric count	= Design height
33	11	= 3in
33	14	= 2½in approx.
33	18	= 1¾in approx.

FABRIC PREPARATION

It is best to prepare your fabric before you start stitching. To prevent fraying whilst stitching, trim the edges of Aida fabric with pinking shears and for evenweaves overcast the edges either by hand or with zigzag stitching by machine. It is preferable to work cross stitch from the centre of the design outwards, as this will ensure that the stitching is always central. To find the centre of the fabric fold it first in half and then into quarters. Lightly crease these folds and then mark the central lines with tacking stitches, which are removed when the work is complete. Match the central square on the chart with the central point on the chart.

THE STITCHES

STARTING AND FINISHING WORK

Do not use a knot to begin and end your cross stitching as knots leave ugly bumps on the finished piece. There are various ways to start but perhaps the simplest is to make the first stitch and leave a 3cm (1¼in) long tail at the back of the fabric. This is then secured by working your first stitches over it.

To change thread or finish off, take the thread to the back of the work and pass it through a few adjacent stitches, away from the edges, for a neat finish.

CROSS STITCH

This is the basic stitch used throughout the book and is shown by a circular symbol within a chart square. Cross stitch is usually worked with two strands of stranded cotton and is very simple to do. When working on Aida, cross stitches are worked diagonally over one block between the holes (see fig 1). When working on an evenweave such as linen, the cross stitches are worked over two threads of the fabric (see fig 2).

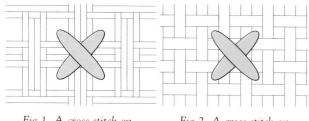

Fig 1 A cross stitch on Aida   Fig 2 A cross stitch on evenweave

To work a whole cross stitch, follow fig 3 below, bringing the needle up from the back of the fabric to the front at (a). Cross diagonally and go down to the back at (b) and come up again at (c). Cross diagonally and go down at (d) to finish the stitch. One golden rule is that the top diagonal stitch should *always* be formed in the same direction.

When covering large areas you may prefer to work cross stitch in rows. To do this, work half a row of cross stitches and then return along the row, completing the cross stitches (see fig 4).

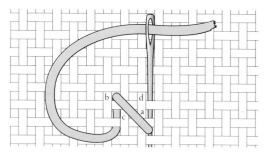

Fig 3 Working a single cross stitch

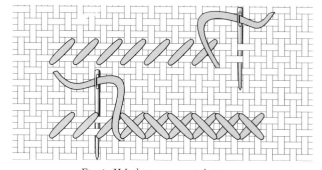

Fig 4 Working cross stitch in rows

THREE-QUARTER CROSS STITCH

Three-quarter cross stitch is used to give detail to a design. It is shown on the charts by a small circular symbol in one quarter of a square. Work the first half of a cross stitch, then work the second stitch across diagonally but taking the needle down through the *centre* hole (see fig 5).

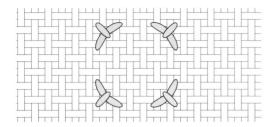

Fig 5 Three-quarter cross stitch

BACKSTITCH

Backstitch is used for outlining a design, highlighting parts of it and for blackwork. It is indicated by a solid thin black line on the charts and usually uses one strand of stranded cotton.

Following fig 6, bring the needle to the front, one block (or two evenweave threads) ahead of the starting point. Make a stitch back to the starting point, then re-emerge one block (or two evenweave threads) ahead of the last completed stitch.

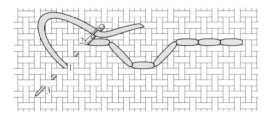

Fig 6 Backstitch

LONG STITCH

Long stitches (see fig 7) are used when a longer stitch than a backstitch is required, such as the kite string on page 24. Long stitches are shown on the charts by a straight coloured line and usually use one strand of stranded cotton, although two strands will give greater emphasis.

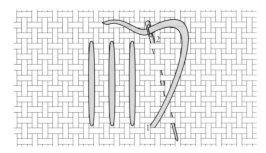

Fig 7 Long stitch

FRENCH KNOTS

French knots are a useful accompaniment to cross stitch. Those on the musical notes chart on page 42 use one strand of stranded cotton. To work, bring the needle up to the front of the fabric and wrap the thread twice around the needle (fig 8). Still holding the thread, return the needle through the fabric one thread or part of a block away, pulling the thread gently to form a loose knot.

Fig 8 French knot

TEN TIPS FOR PERFECT STITCHING

- Use a good pair of embroidery scissors with sharp points for cutting threads – essential for a neat finish.
- Use a length of thread no more than 18in (46cm) long in order to prevent tangles.
- All the top diagonal stitches in cross stitch should lie in the same direction for a neat finish.
- Do not pull the stitches too tightly, they should sit 'graciously' on the fabric.
- Drop your needle every now and then and let it spin, this will take the twists out and so avoid infuriating tangles.
- Do not carry threads across an open expanse of fabric: finish off and begin again. Loose threads, particularly dark ones, will be visible from the right side when the work is complete.
- When working on dark fabrics it is hard to see the holes. Use a white pillowcase or similar over your knee and the holes will show up more clearly.
- Look after your eyes by using a daylight bulb for night-time stitching, a magnifier when the fabric is fine and take regular breaks, every twenty minutes or so, to rest and readapt your vision. The benefit is fewer mistakes.
- If you are using several small designs to make up a larger picture, plan the whole design before you begin stitching. Photocopy the design charts, cut out the shapes and position them on a large piece of paper or graph paper and use this as your guide.
- Don't leave needles in fabric or fabric in hoops for any length of time, to avoid marking and creasing your work.

PERIOD STYLE

HIS CHAPTER is full of timeless motifs reminis-
cent of the past, all ideal for decorating items for
the home and to give as gifts. There are elegant profile
portraits reflecting historical periods and lovely floral
motifs from a romantic age, attractive alone or for
embellishing other designs. There is also a selection
of ecclesiastical, heraldic and Celtic motifs all evoking
past ages and perfect for more formal, symmetrical
designs. When making up items refer to Finishing and
Making Up.

× × × × × ×   *Stitching notes*   × × × × × ×

*Period style portraits decorate a lovely dressing
table set of silver mirror and hair brush (from Framecraft).
The Victorians loved silhouettes and used a blend of
brown and black on pale backgrounds for soft and gentle
images. Reflecting this idea, cream 18 count Aida has been
used for the set, stitched with two strands of very dark grey
stranded cotton. The silver trinket pot (from Framecraft) is
inset with a delicate posy in very dark grey on cream 18
count Aida. Exotic fuchsias stitched in the same grey over
two threads of a cream 28 count evenweave fabric look
stunning when made into a bag, perfect for a pot-pourri
holder, a make-up bag or cotton wool store (see page 122
for making the bag). A distinctive Celtic design in very
dark grey on cream 28 count linen, made up into a
bookmark will ensure that you never lose your place.*

× ×

VARIATIONS ON A THEME

■ Children at play, stitched as pictures using cross stitch
and backstitch, would enliven any hall or staircase. Any
of the antique-style vehicles could be used for an office
desk tidy. The Celtic and ecclesiastical designs would
make stunning book covers or cards. The heraldic
shields could be stitched over one thread of 22 count
Hardanger fabric with one strand of gold or deep red and
used to cover buttons to add style to a jacket or coat.

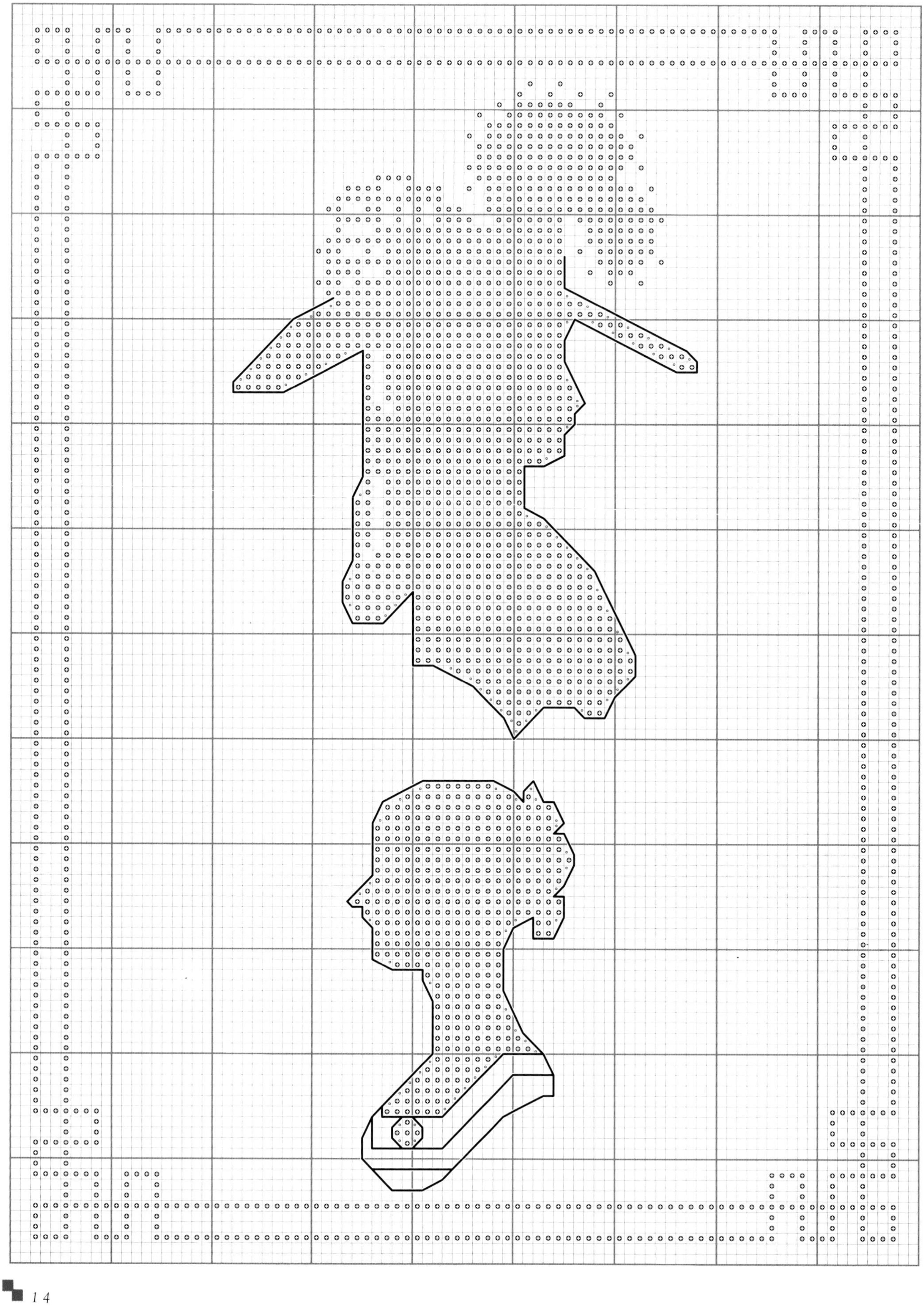

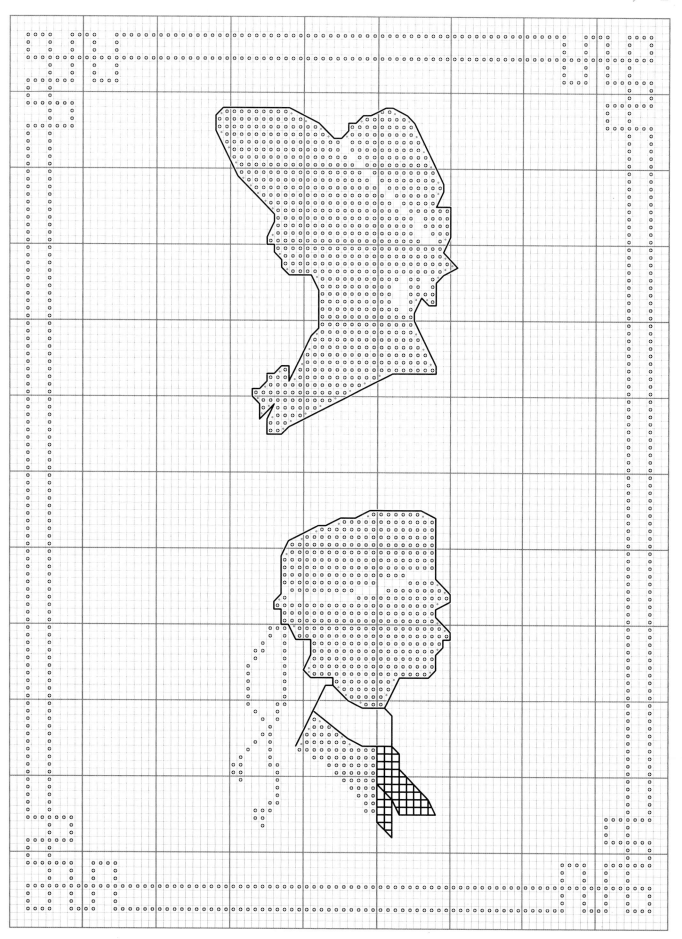

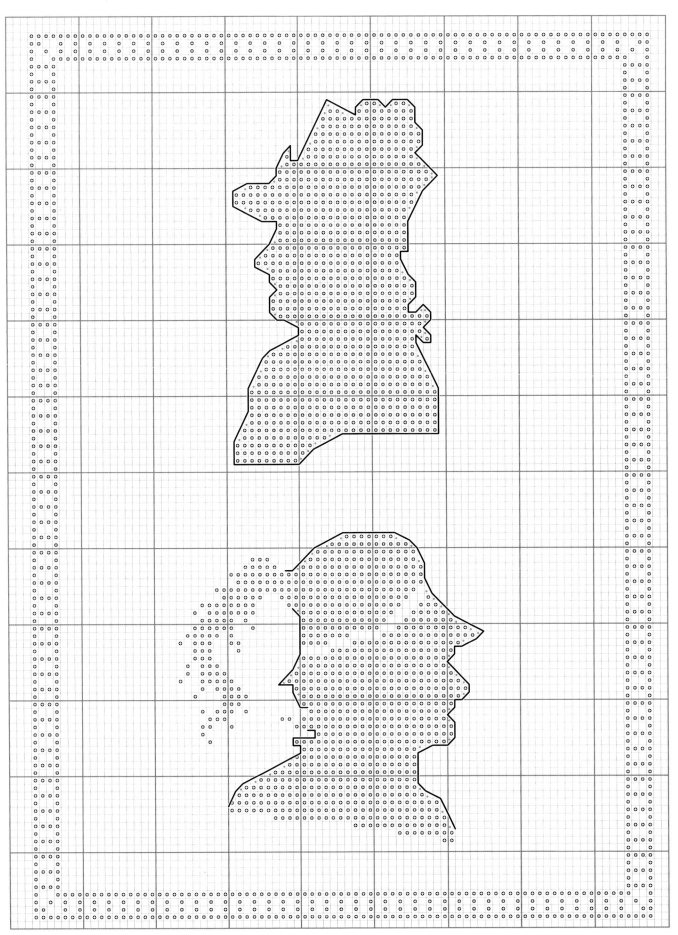

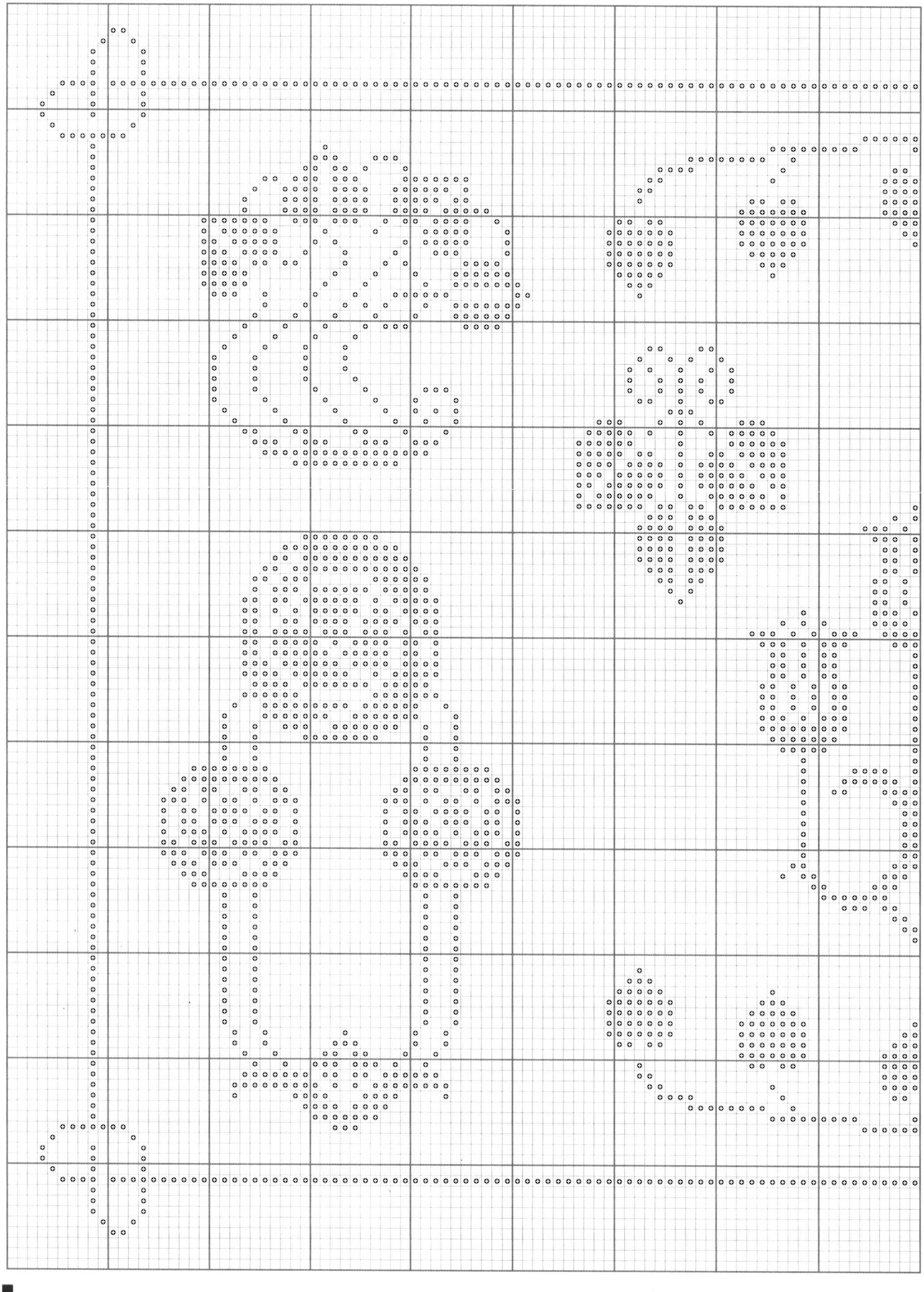

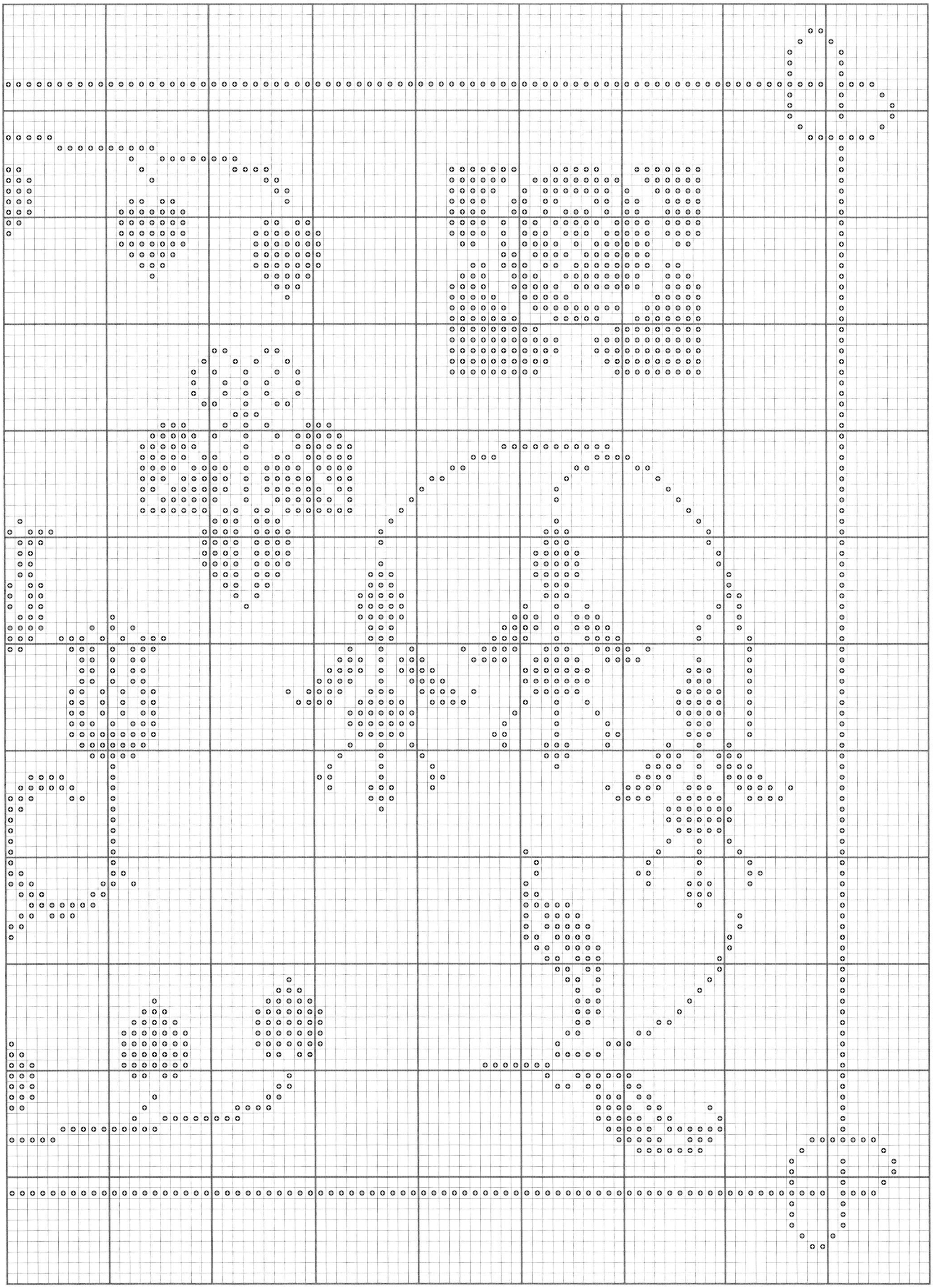

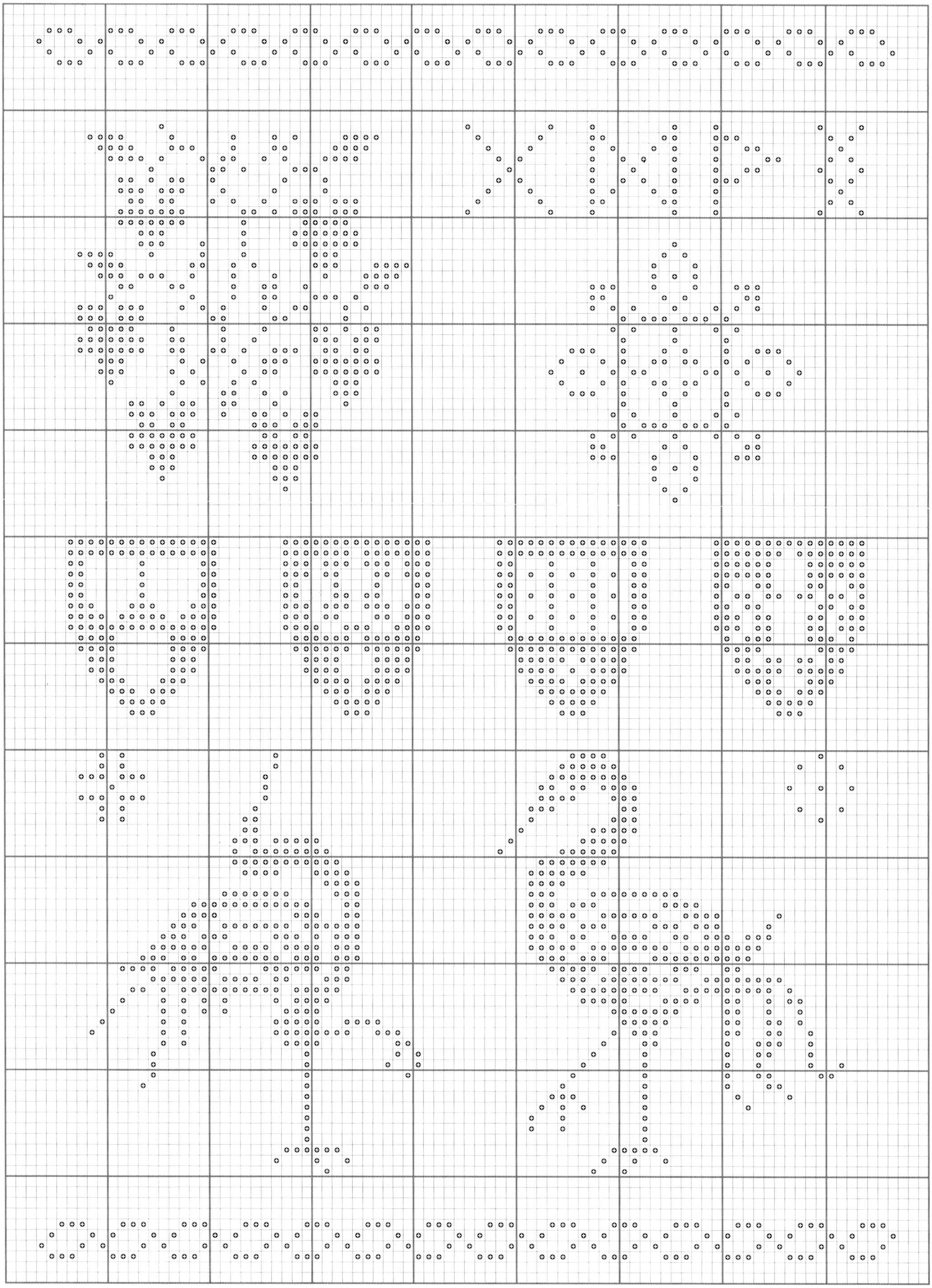

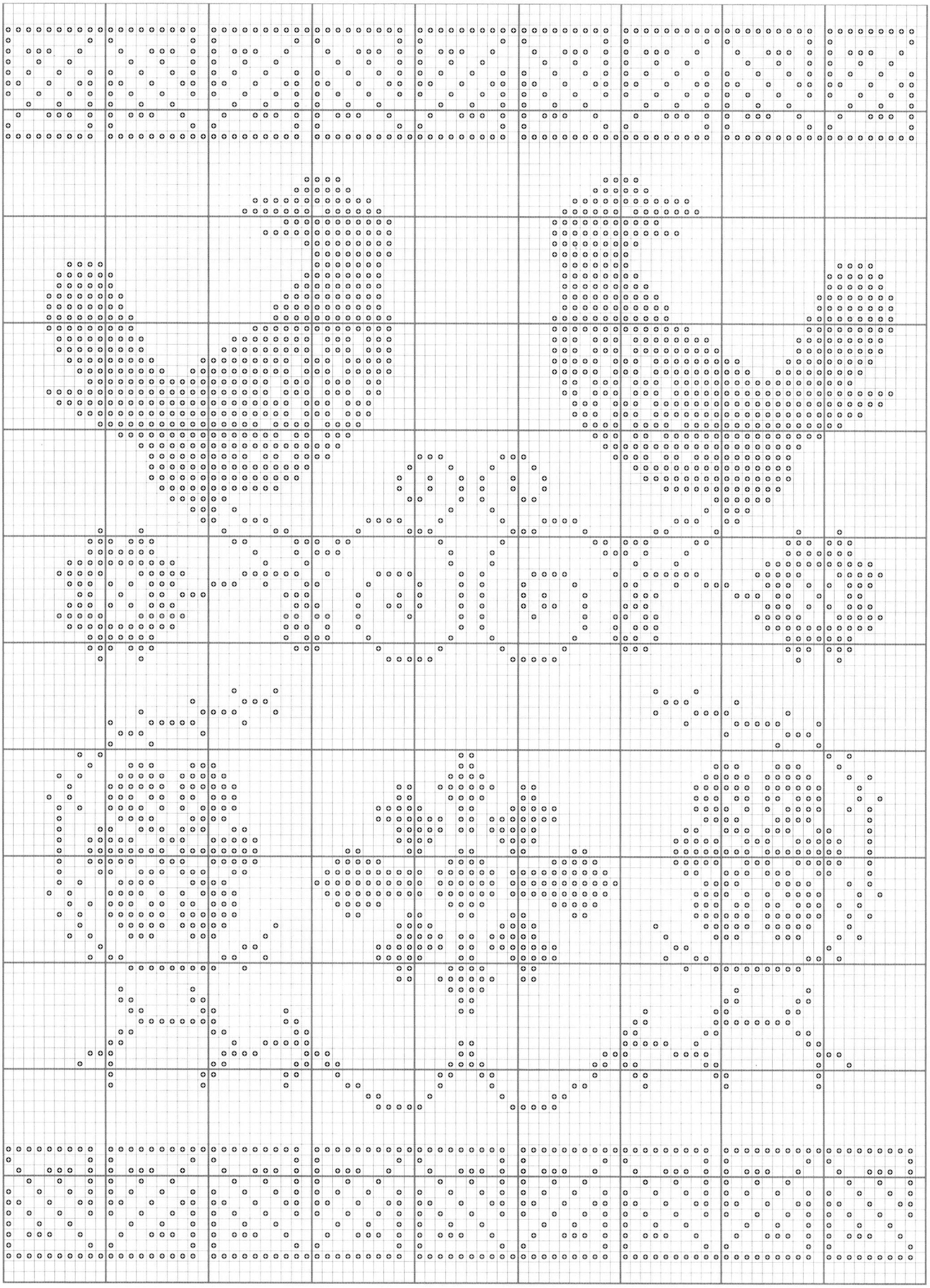

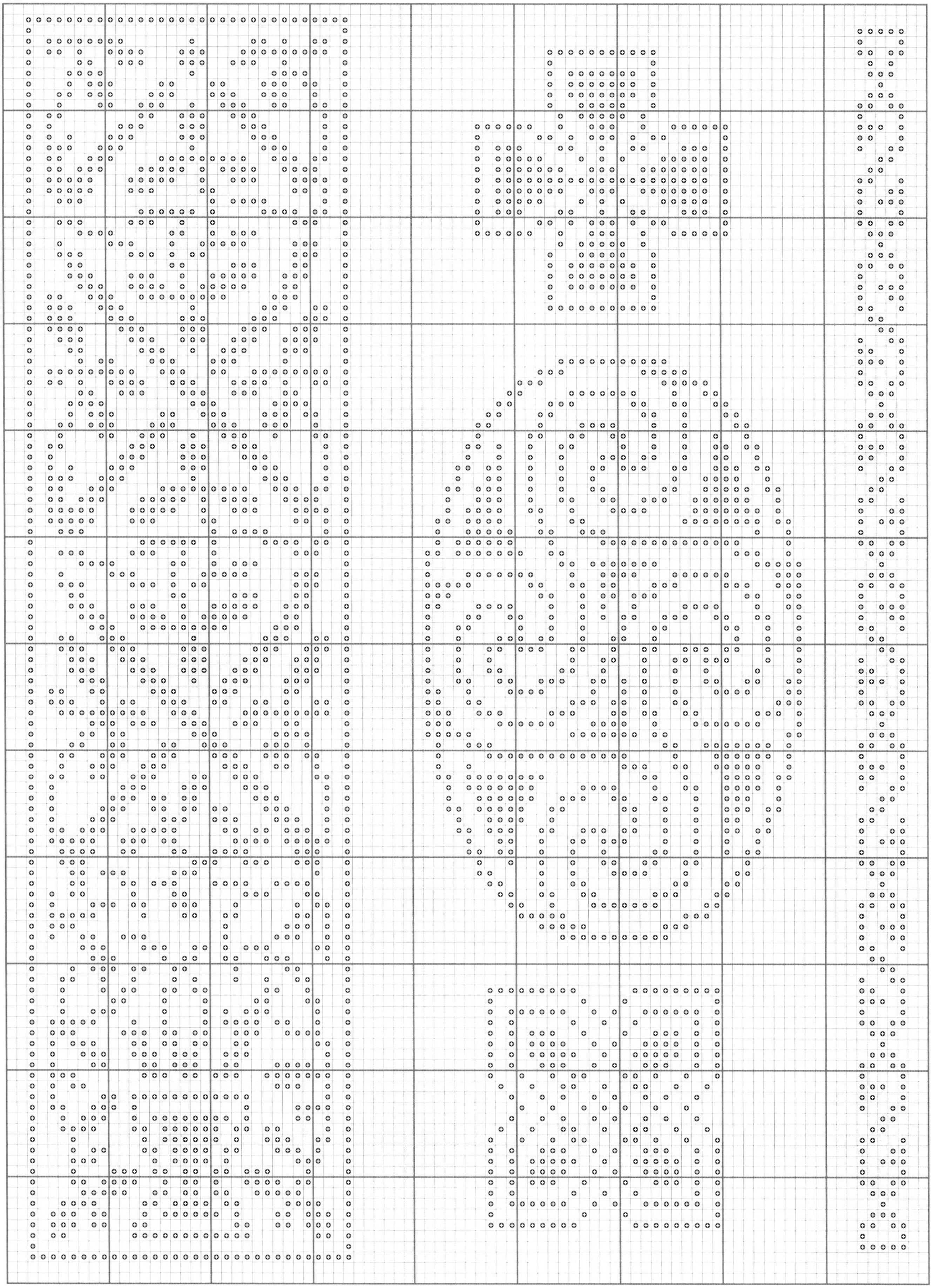

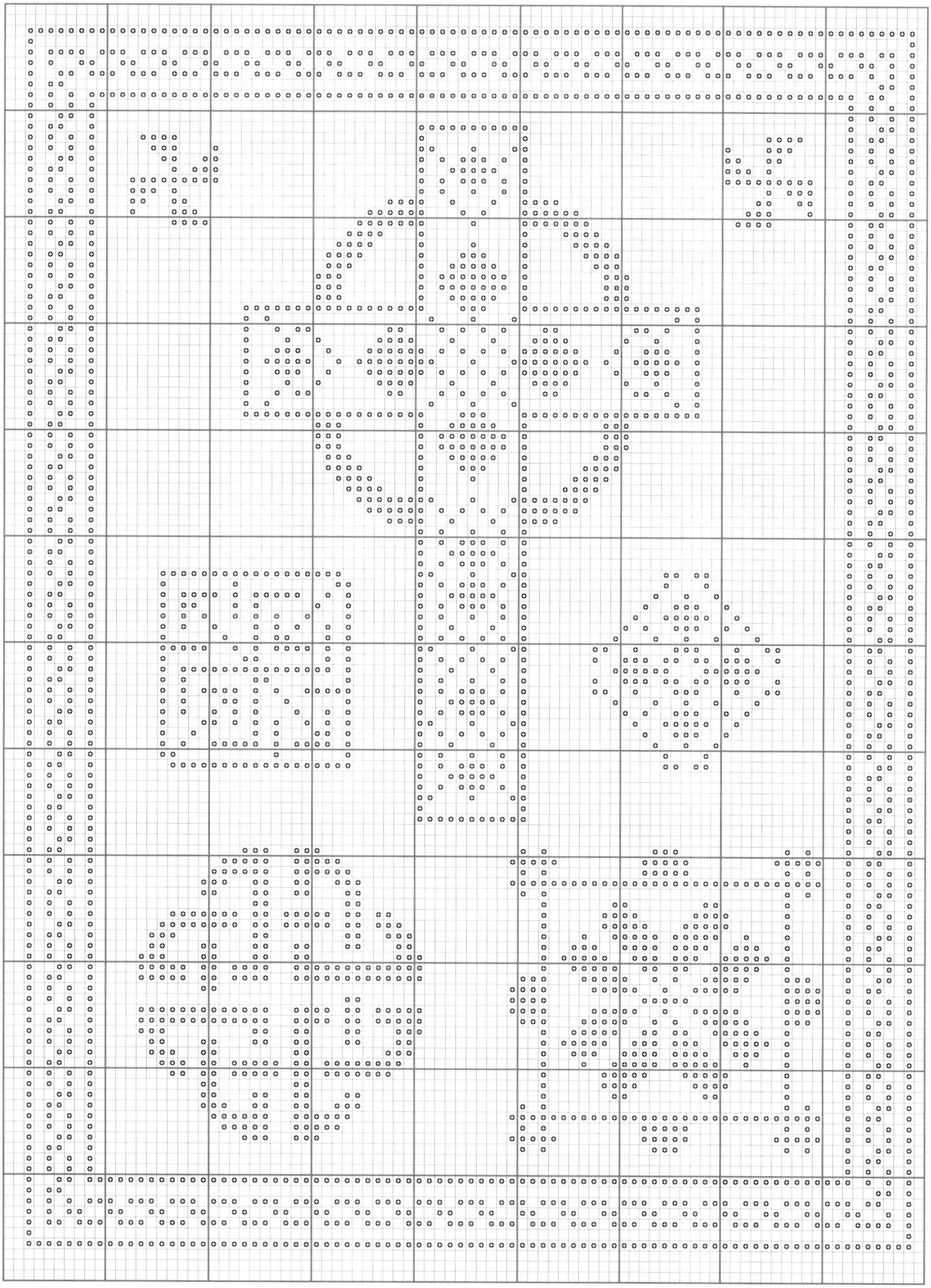

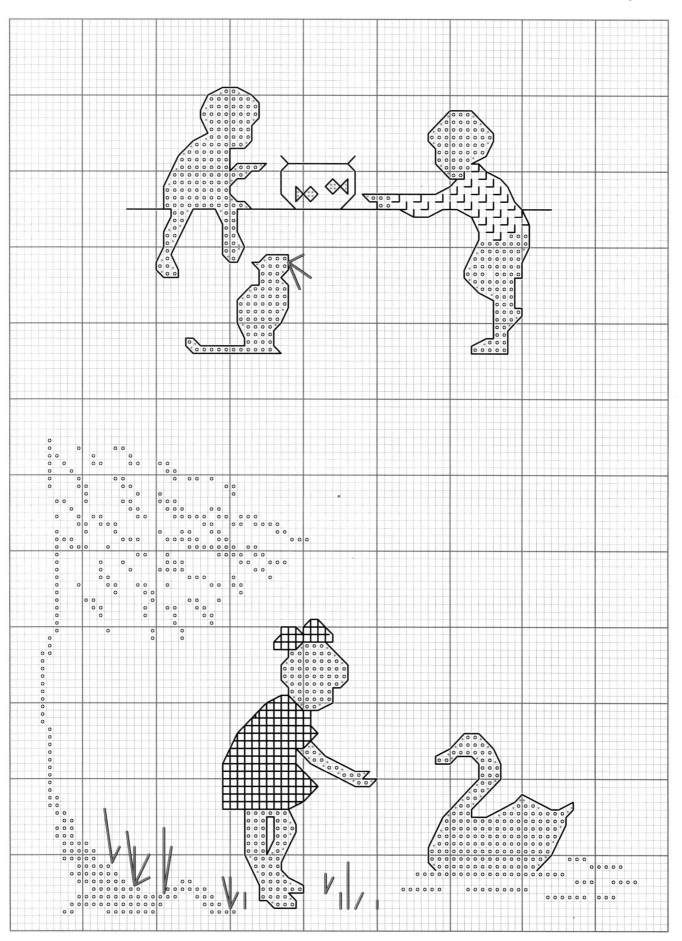

COUNTRY CHARMS

E VOCATIVE SCENES from the countryside feature in this chapter, including two dreamy riverside views with heron, otter, willow, bulrushes and kingfisher. Woodland animals among trees include squirrel, rabbit and deer – lively motifs to feature on many household items. Farmyard creatures such as a sow and her piglets and a cockerel and hens can be used in a picture scene or individually. When making up projects refer to Finishing and Making Up.

× × × × × *Stitching notes* × × × × ×

A delightful farmyard scene adorns the pocket of a navy blue apron. Stitched on 28 count cream linen it uses one strand of ruby Wildflower thread by Caron. A cheeky squirrel has been stitched on cream 18 count Aida with two strands of golden brown thread to match the wooden trinket box from Framecraft. The riverside walk has been worked with two strands of A128 Bravo variegated thread from Rainbow Gallery. The natural tones produce a watery effect when stitched onto denim blue Jobelan fabric, while a pine frame completes the picture. A pretty metal frame makes an interesting mount for a water scene featuring delicate dragonflies and irises. The design is stitched on cream 18 count Aida in one strand of Caron Royal Jewels Wildflower thread. A natural-coloured box, useful for storing needlework accessories, has a central aperture featuring a horse and carriage stitched with one strand of dark brown stranded cotton onto cream 18 count Aida.

× ×

VARIATIONS ON A THEME

■ The stylish horse and carriage design would make a splendid gift if worked as a piece for a tray or workbox. Any of the motifs from the woodland scene could be stitched as single items and used in cards or coasters. A selection of farmyard animals would make attractive pictures for a country kitchen. Butterflies stitched in bright variegated threads would look most effective in display cases, available from Framecraft.

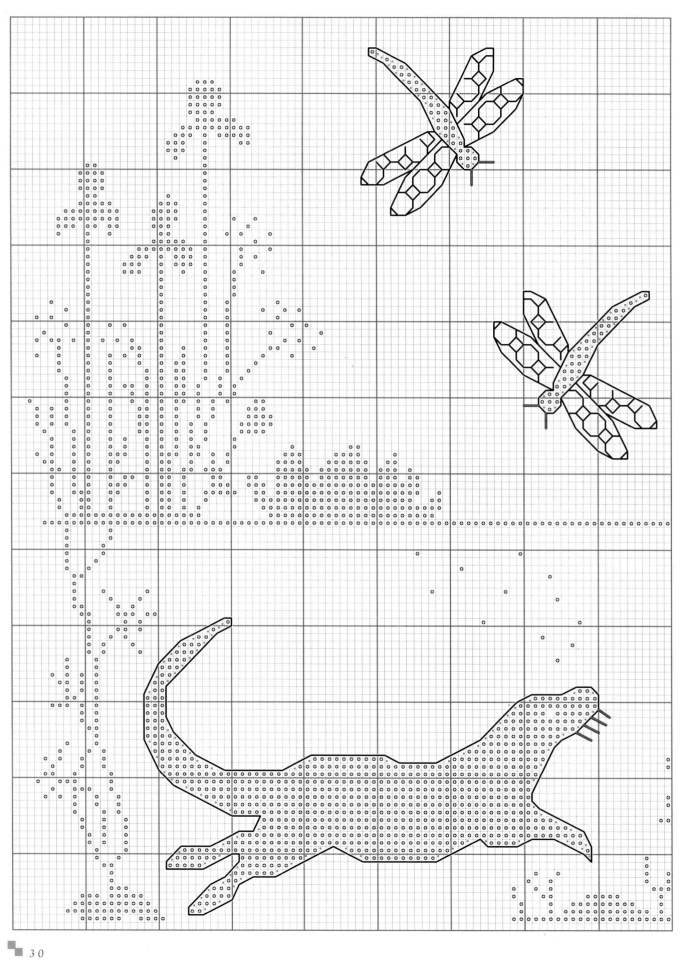

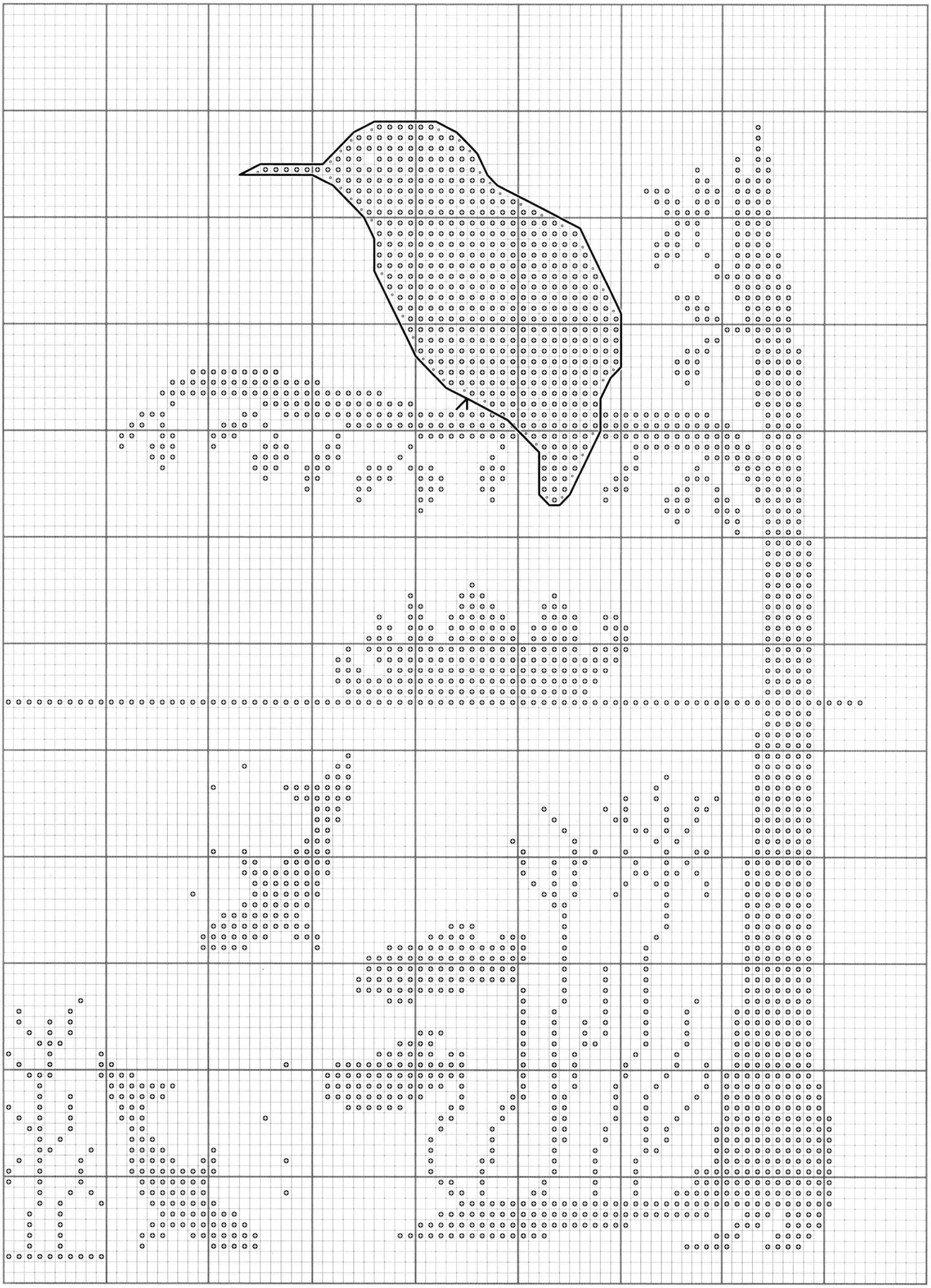

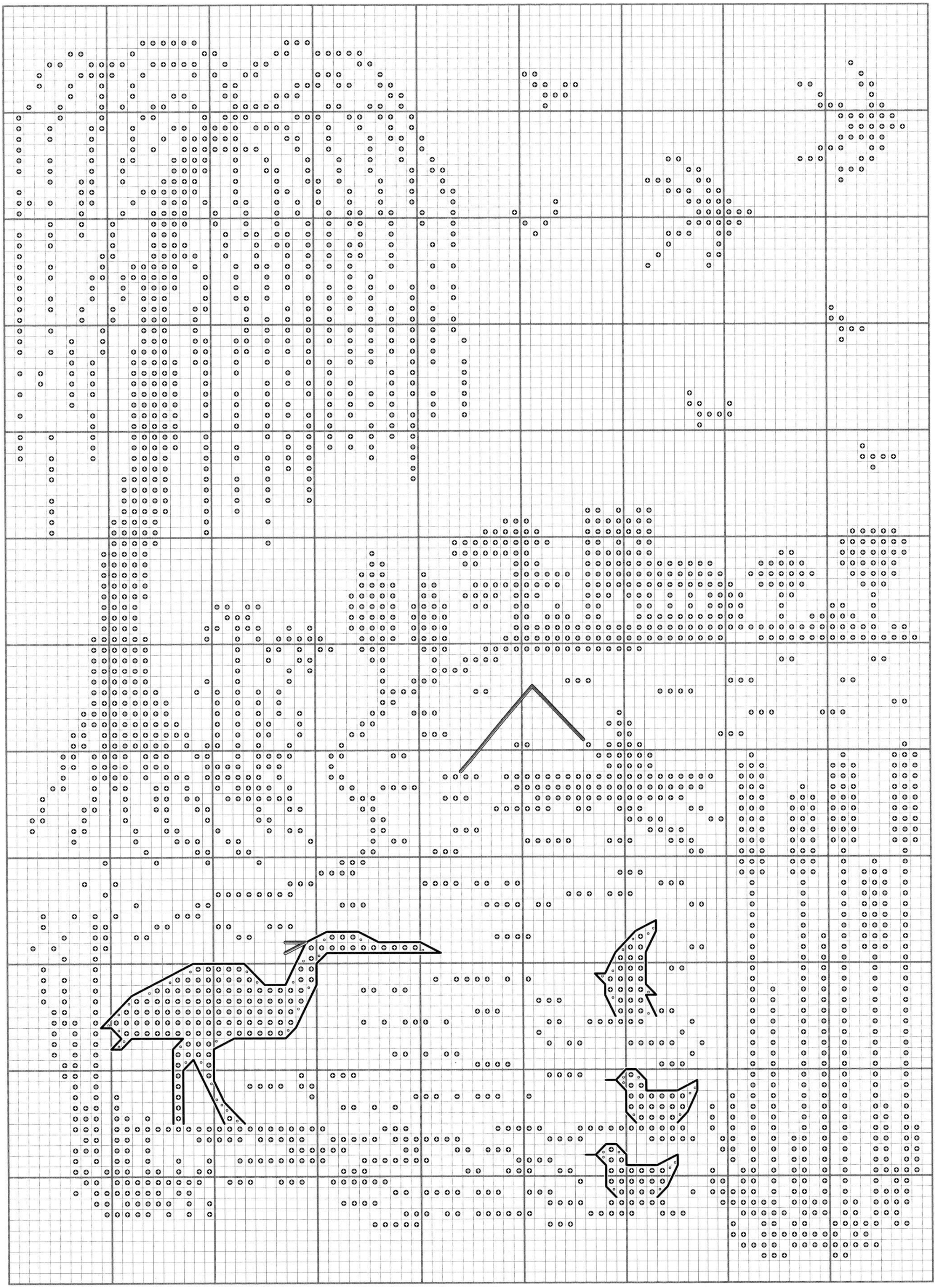

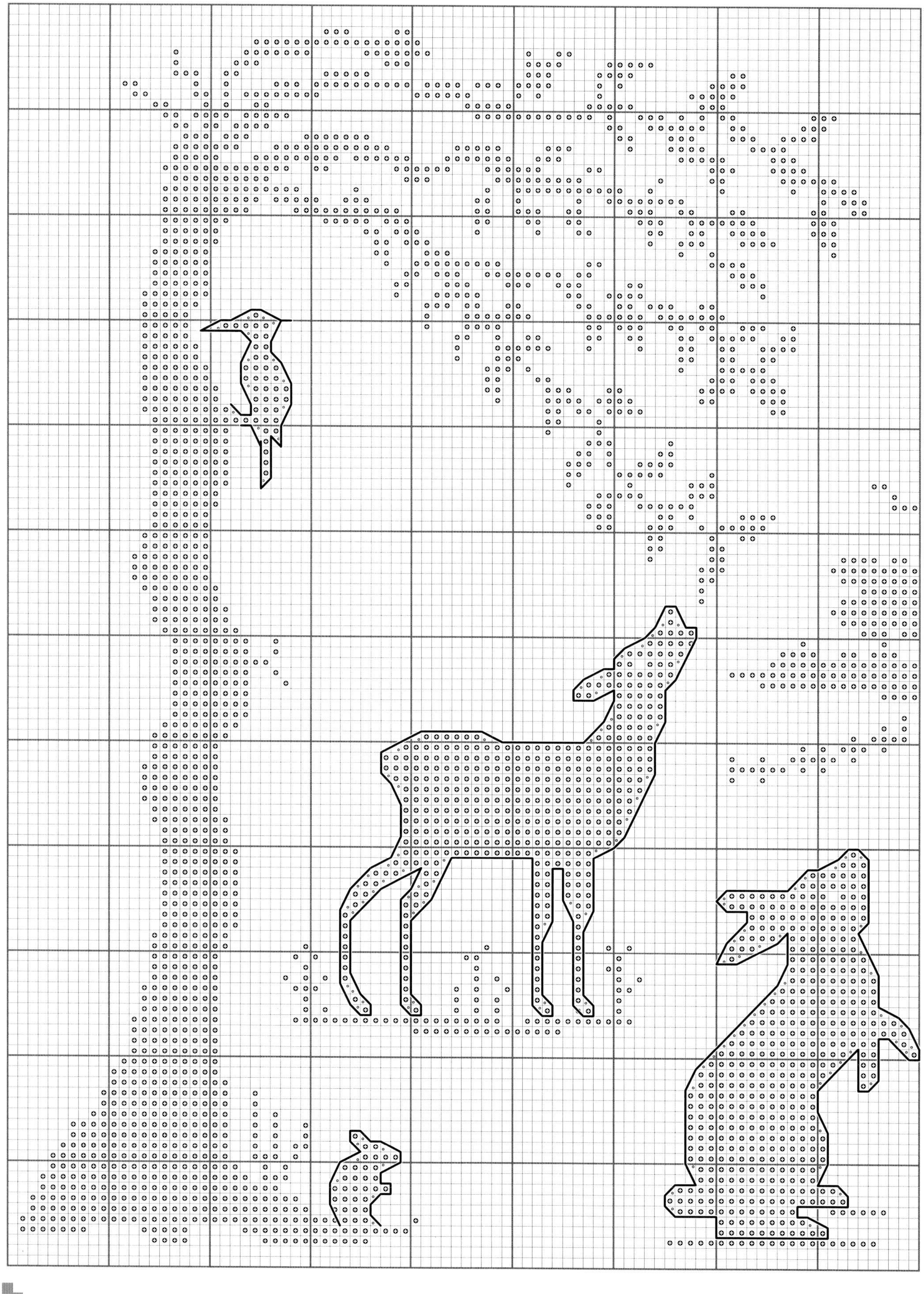

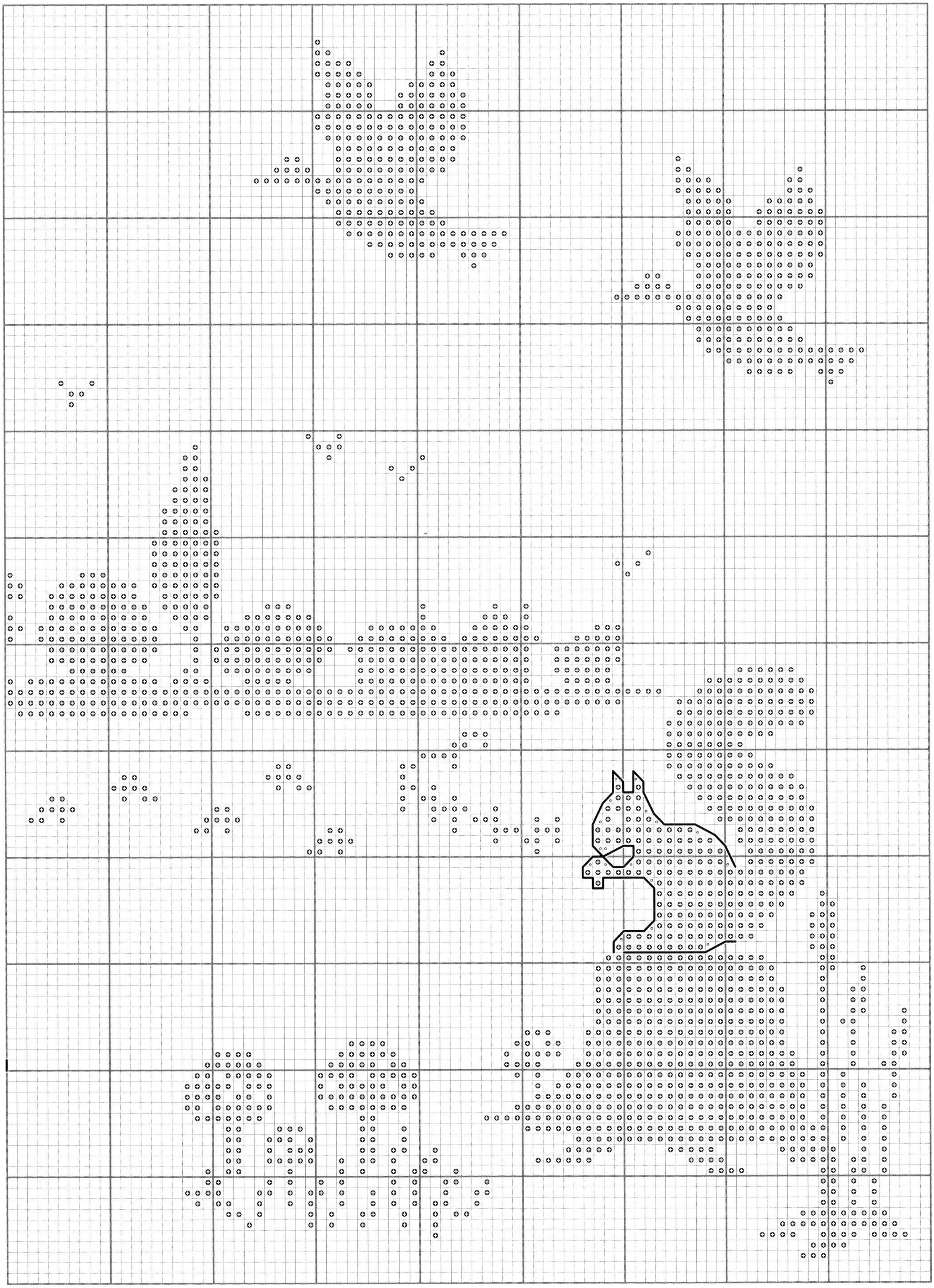

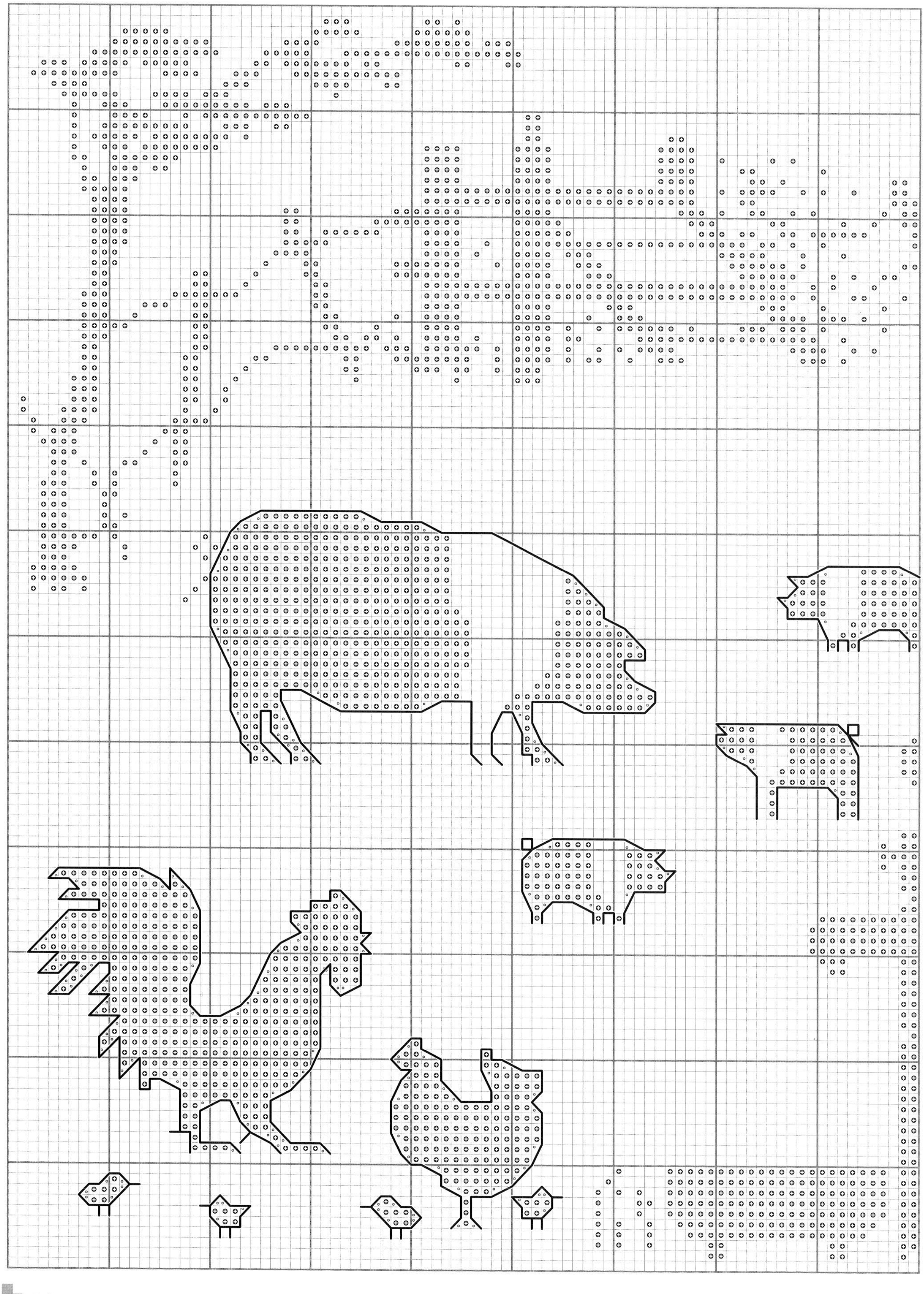

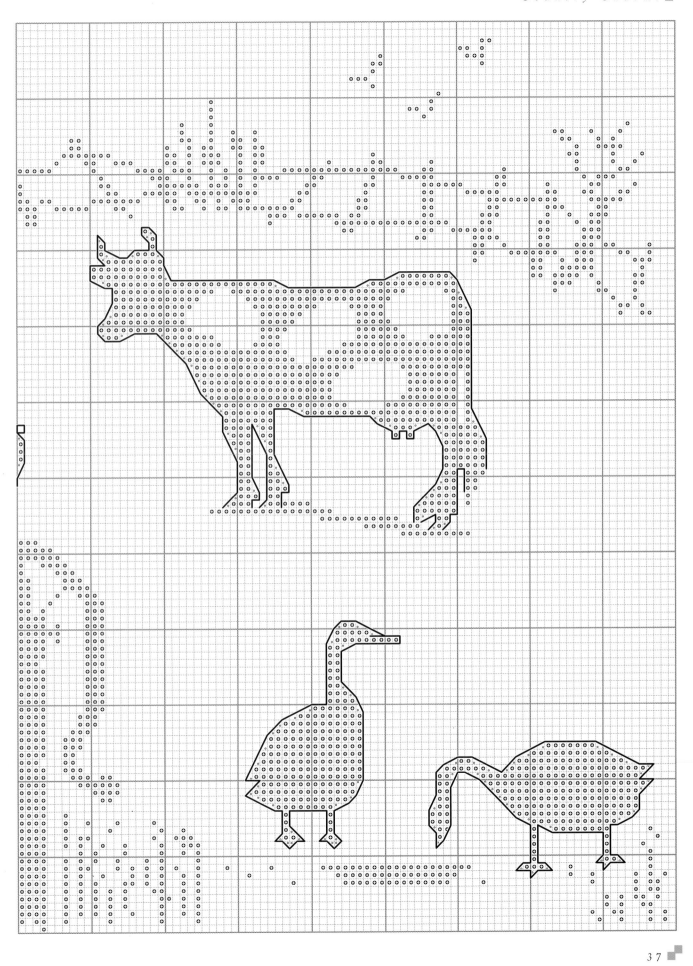

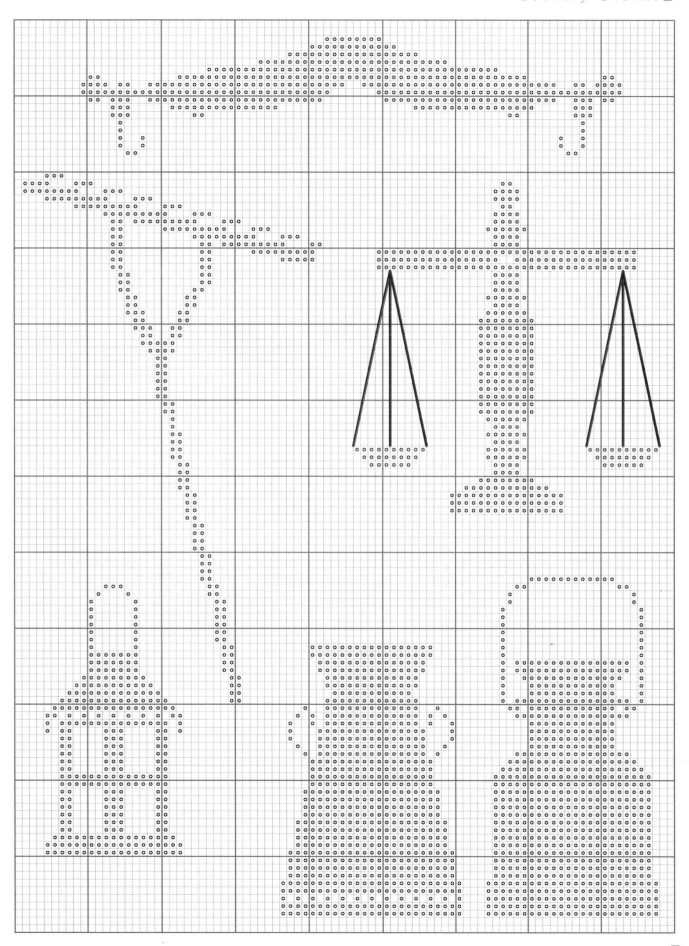

FAVOURITE PASTIMES

T HIS CHAPTER is packed with memorable motifs of favourite pastimes. For the hobbyist there are sewing and gardening motifs; the musician has a wonderful range of musical instruments; for the cook there is a scrumptious selection of kitchen motifs (see picture on page 5). Those keen on sport will find the sports equipment, sporting figures and nautical motifs perfect for decorating all sorts of items. Some of the projects use a 28 count Jobelan fabric, which should be stitched over two threads. When making up projects refer to Finishing and Making Up.

Stitching notes

For the golfing enthusiast, a period-style golfer is perfect for decorating an address book or diary from Framecraft. Stitched with two strands of mid grey stranded cotton on a light grey Jobelan fabric, the grey reflects the muted tones of the William Morris cover. Musical motifs have been arranged in sampler style and framed for budding musicians. The picture has been stitched traditionally on cream Jobelan fabric with two strands of very dark grey stranded cotton. An ideal gift for avid gardeners is an envelope purse to hold all those half-used seed packets. Using a horticultural theme, several garden motifs have been stitched with two strands of dark green stranded cotton onto the purse which is made from pale green Jobelan fabric. A pincushion using patchwork motifs can be seen on page 125.

VARIATIONS ON A THEME

■ Use any of the sporting designs in a card for a sporting enthusiast. Kitchen motifs could decorate tablemats, napkin rings or coasters in colours to complement your home. Patchwork quilt squares could be stitched into a line to embellish a pillow edge or a salt box. The gardening motifs mounted into fridge magnets could be a reminder of gardening jobs to be done. The musical motifs could be stitched on a pincushion, card or brooch.

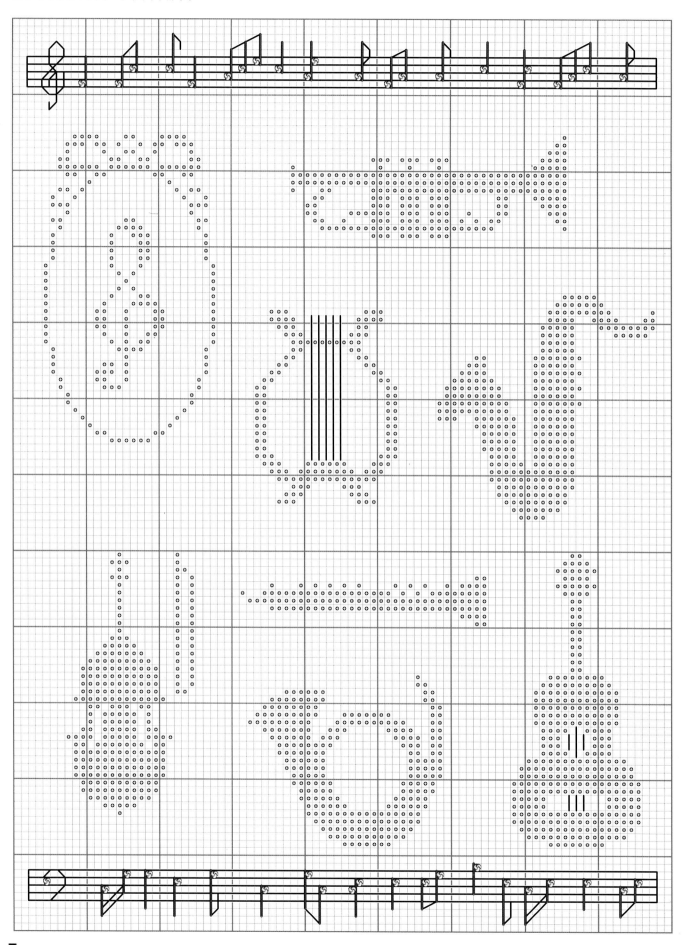

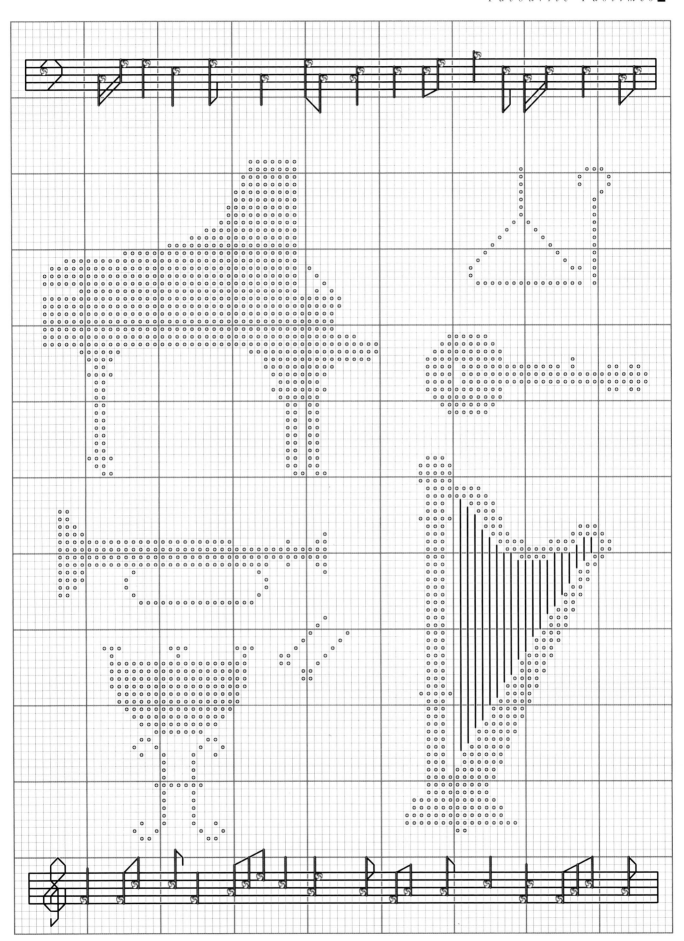

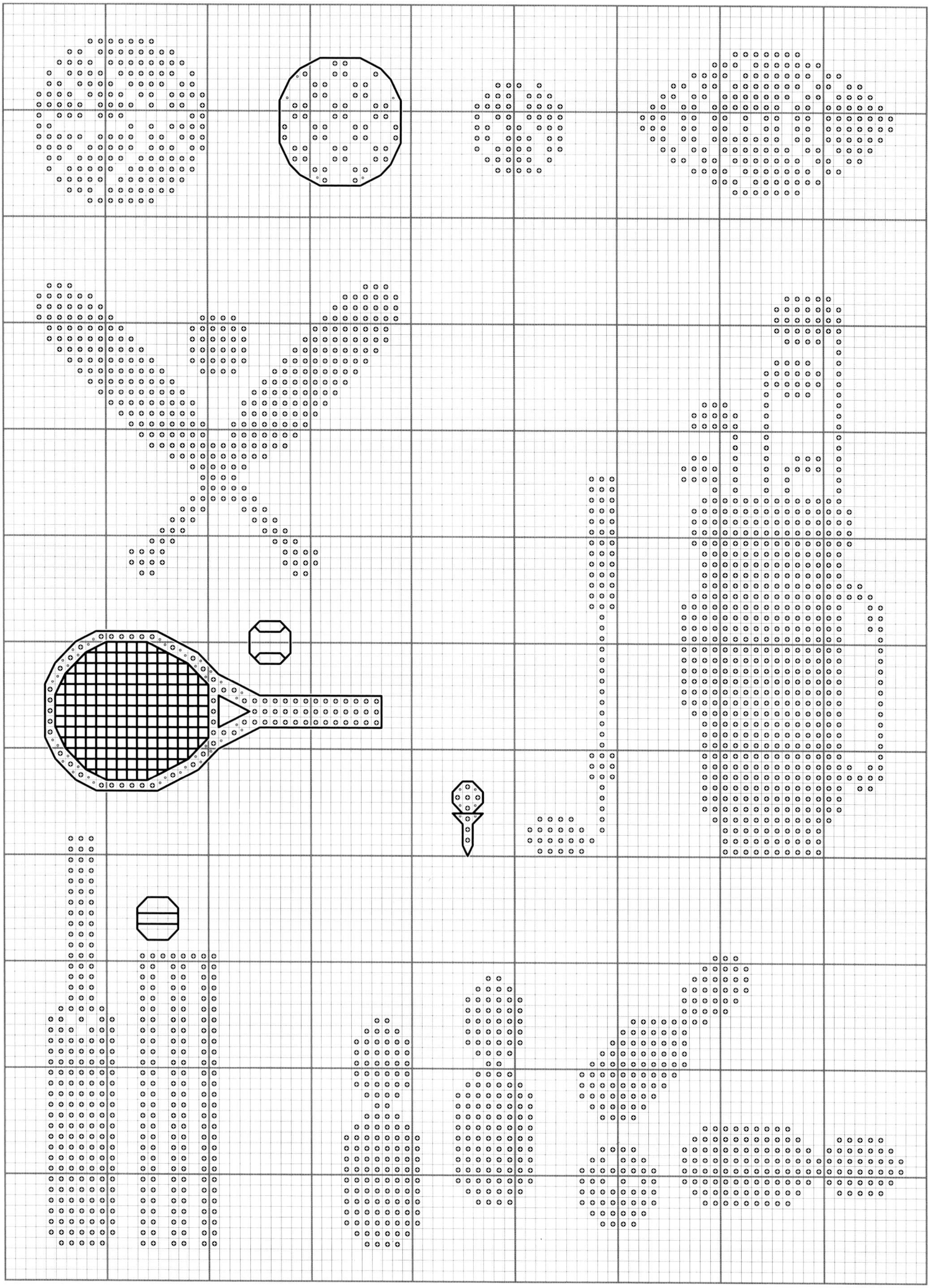

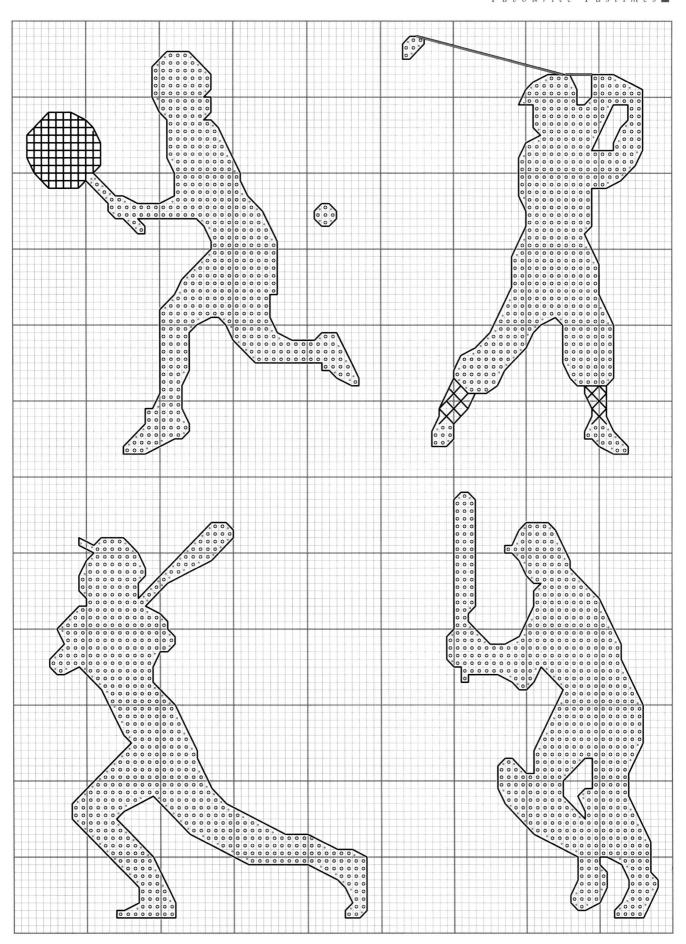

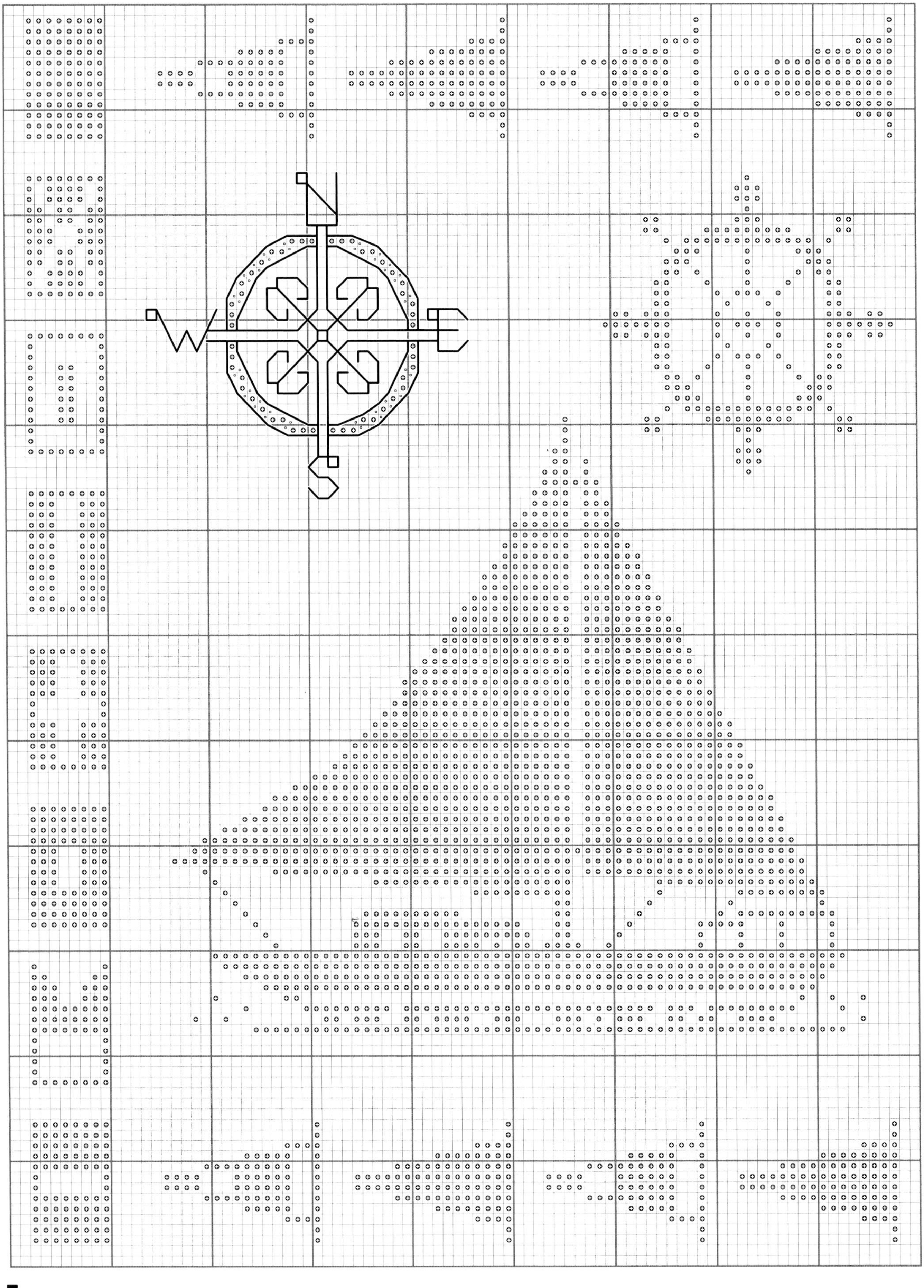
N
W
E
S

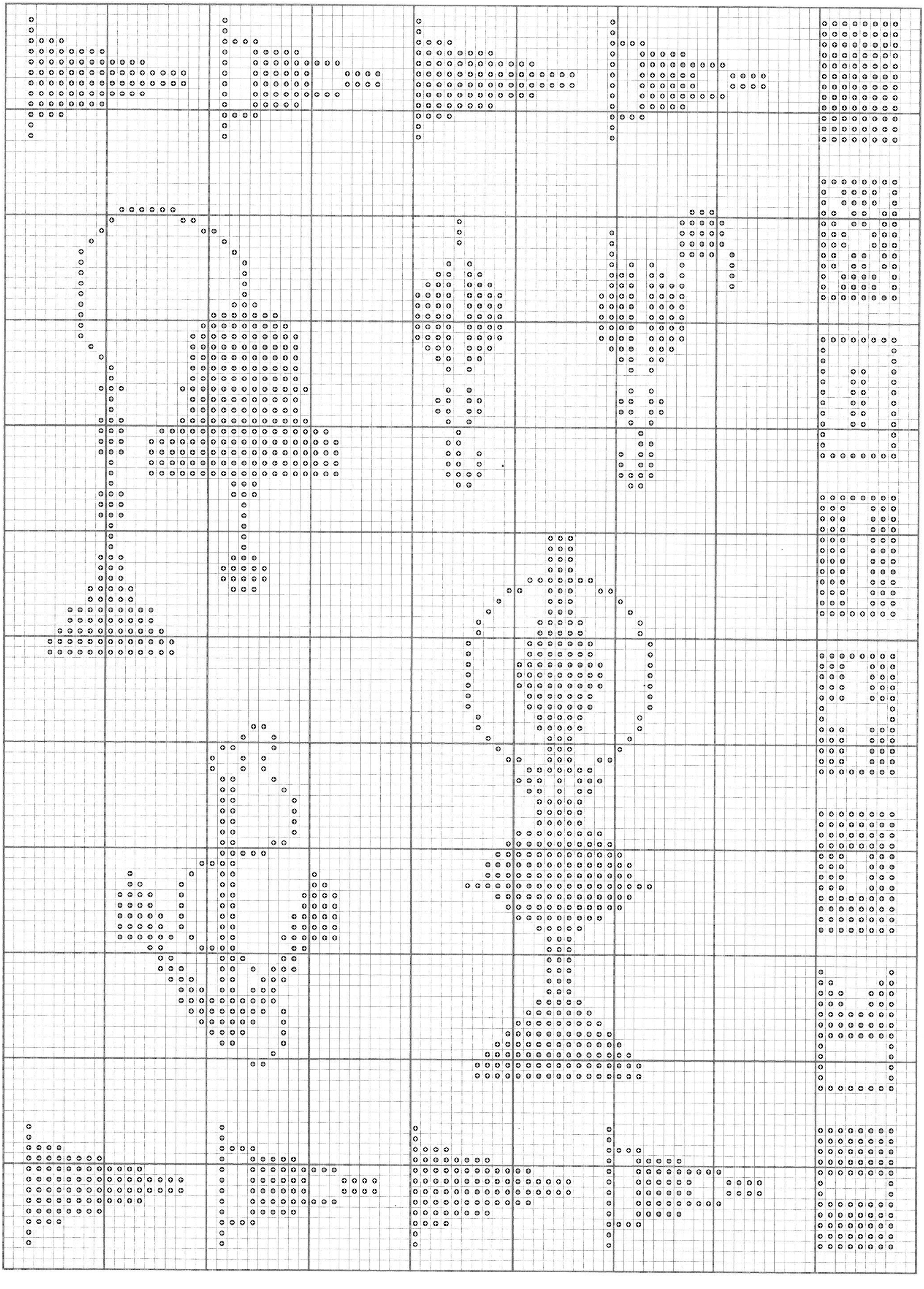

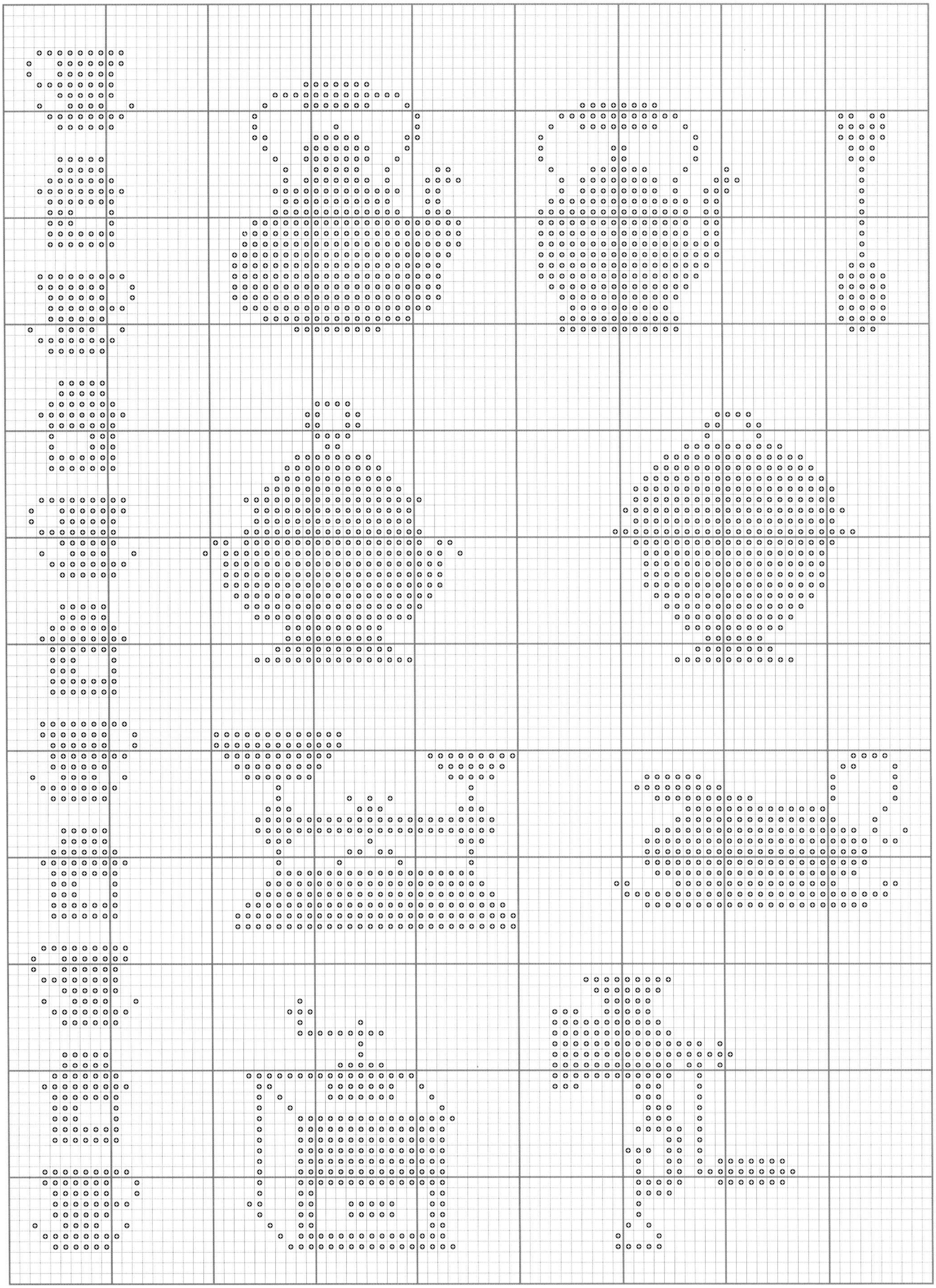

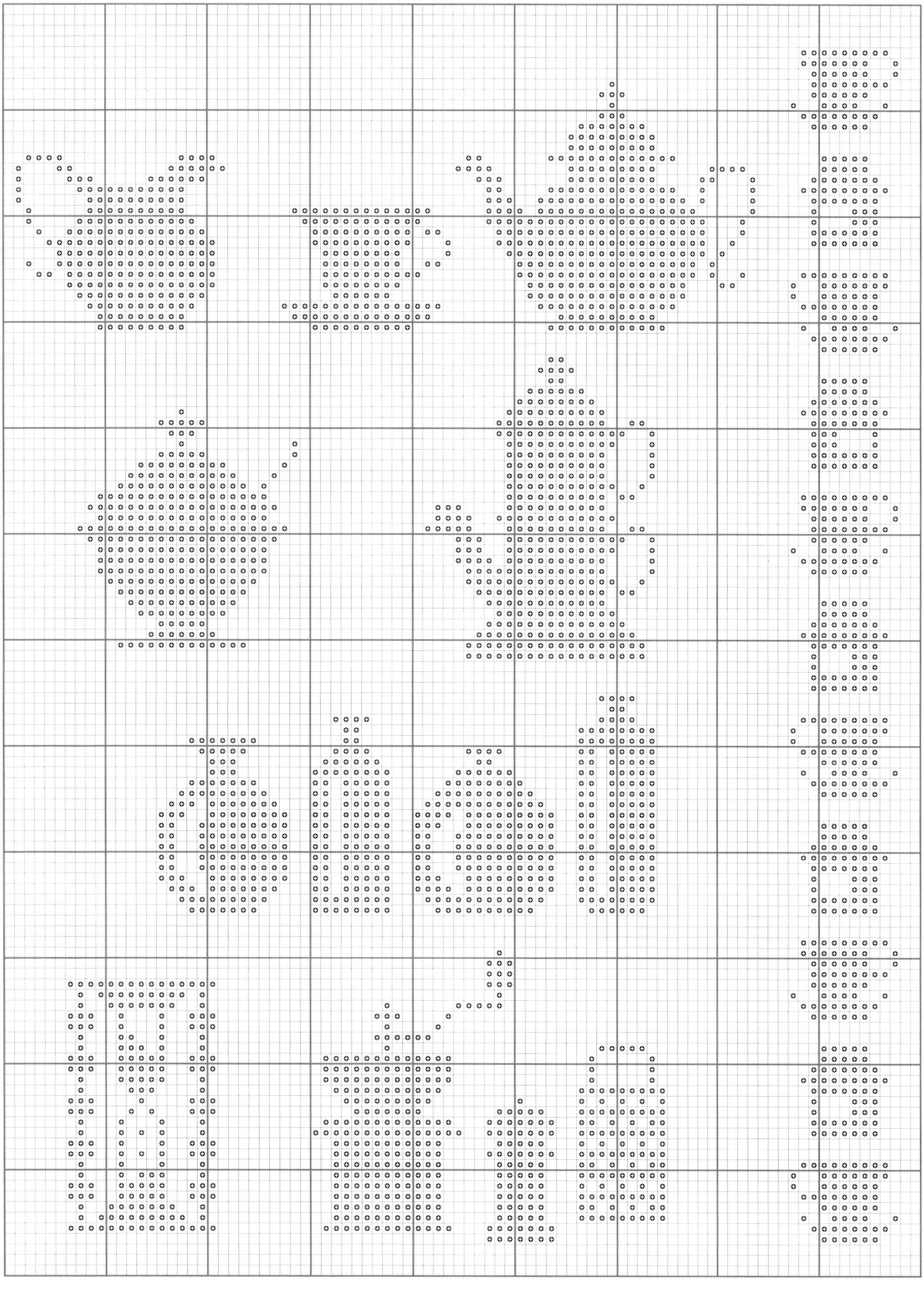

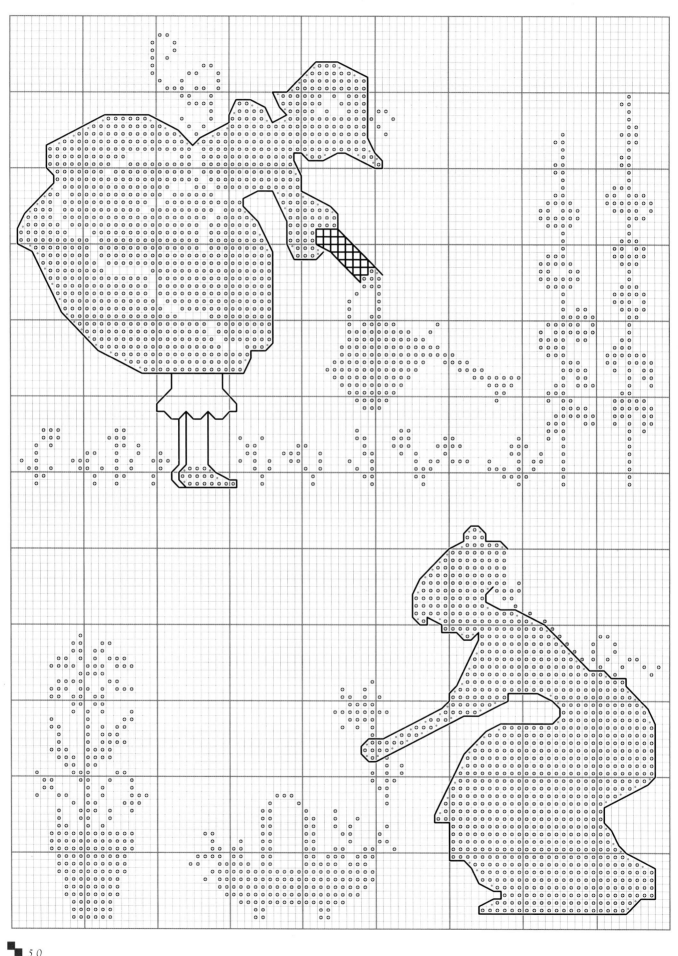

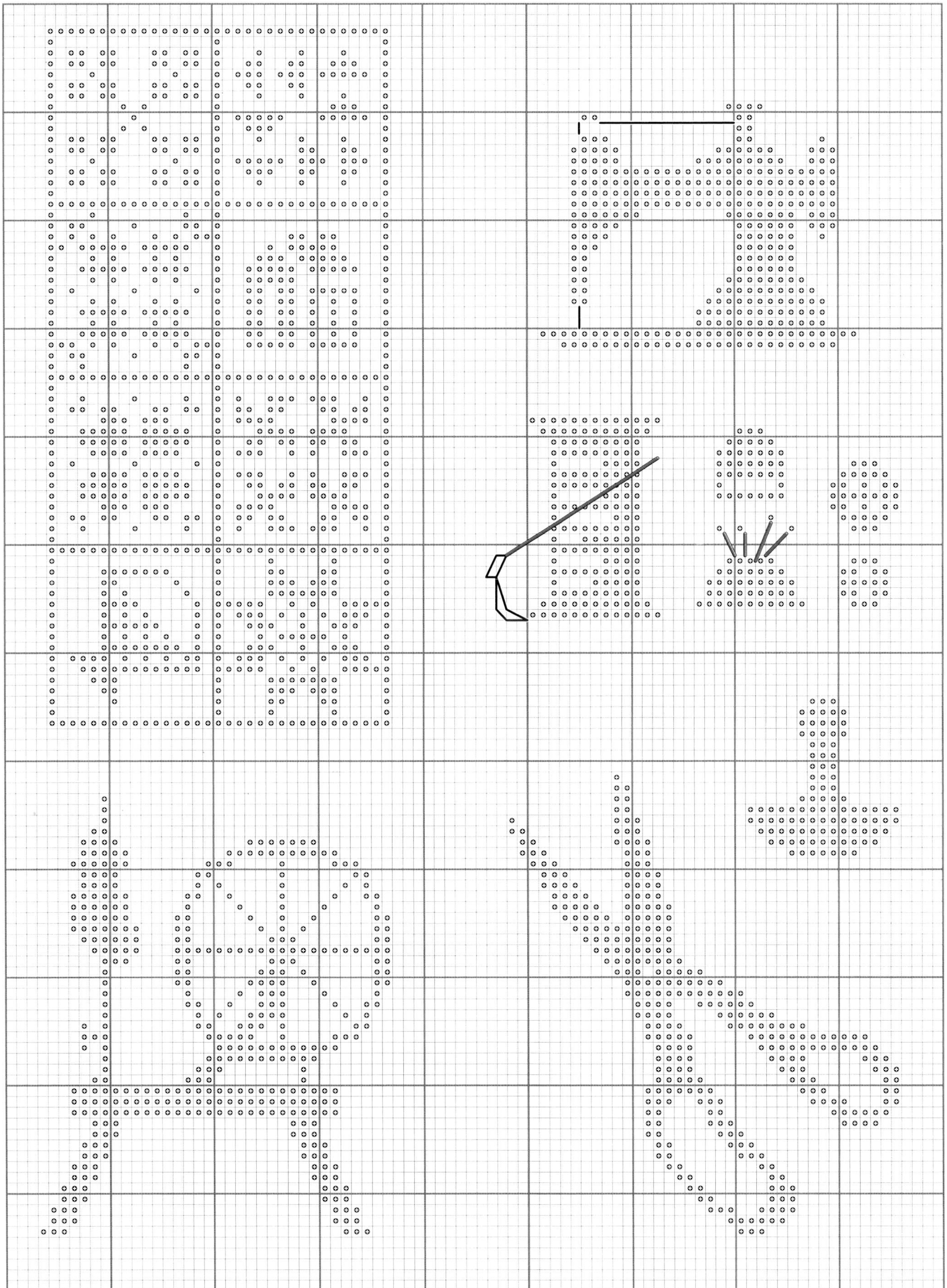

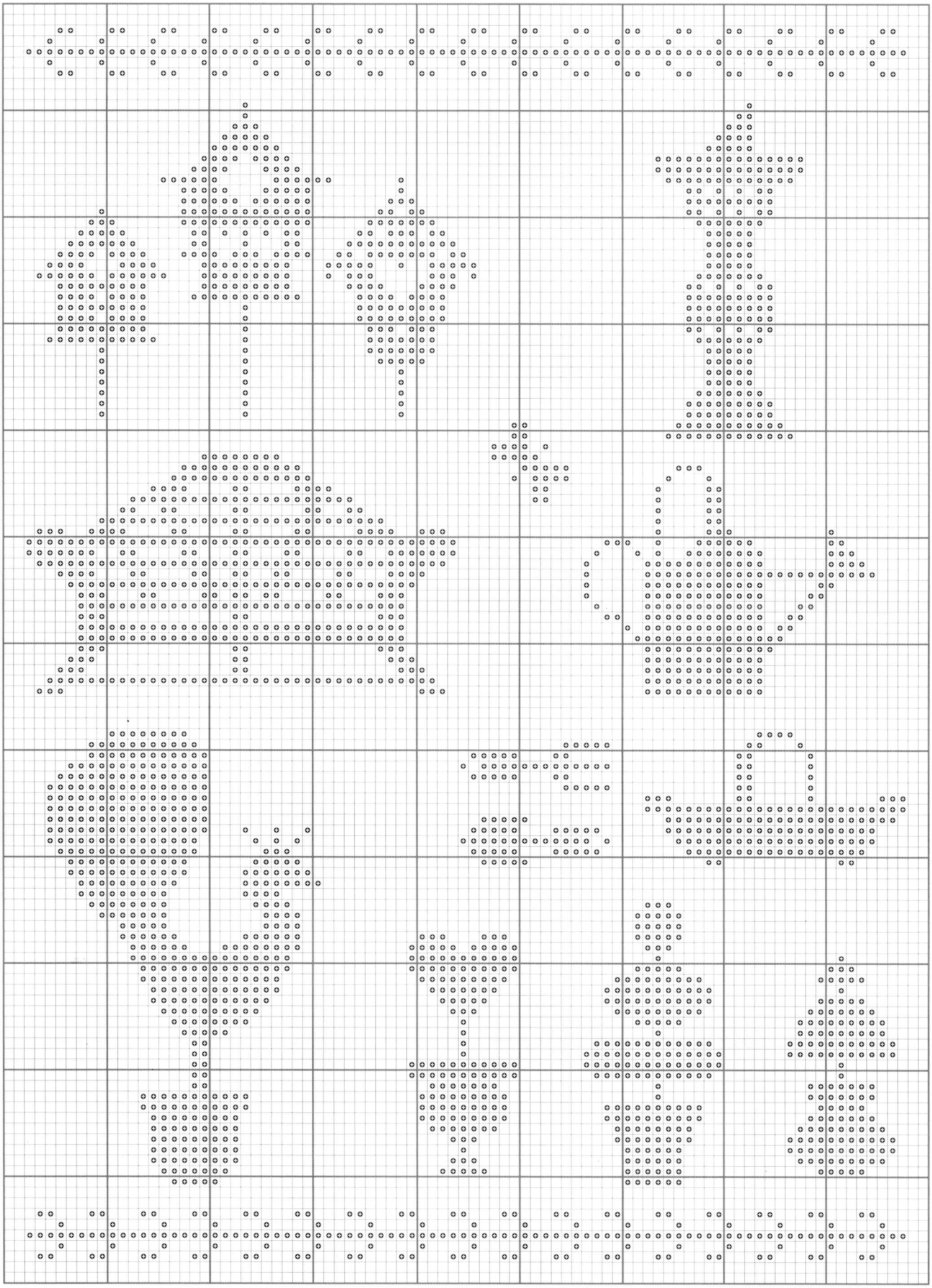

CHILDHOOD CLASSICS

R ETURN TO CHILDHOOD with these delightful designs. Stitching notes are given on page 4 and a picture on page 2, for a cupboard, money-box and sun hat, while a teddy mobile, nightdress case and wizard toy bag are described here. There are many designs to choose from in this chapter including sea-side motifs, fairytale designs, Noah's Ark, the funfair, sporting teddies and playful mice. These themes have been enjoyed by children for centuries and they could stitch many small designs themselves on a large count Aida. The Jobelan fabric used on items shown is a 28 count. When making up projects refer to Finishing and Making Up.

x x x x x x *Stitching notes* x x x x x x

Sporting teddies have been stitched traditionally with two strands of dark grey stranded cotton on cream Jobelan for early recognition: here they are transformed into a wonderful nursery mobile. Paws are stitched on the reverse, on black Jobelan with a blend of one strand of white thread and two strands of Kreinik blending filament 052F which will glow in the dark. Fairies at the bottom of the garden are caught in cross stitch on this adorable souvenir or nightdress case, and envelope type bag, which has been stitched with mauve stranded cotton onto English rose Jobelan. Keep toys tidy in this useful wizard toy sack, the central panel of which is a mystical wizard complete with moon and stars stitched on black Jobelan with a blend of white and metallic silver threads for extra sparkle.

x x x x x x x x x x x x x x x x x x x x x x x x

VARIATIONS ON A THEME

■ Instead of the wizard, stitch the fantastic winged horse Pegasus on the toy sack. Beach huts in red would look good stitched through waste canvas directly onto a child's T. shirt or beach bag. The seaside designs are wonderfully rewarding projects for children to stitch, particularly the tug boat and lighthouse, worked on a 6, 8 or 11 count Aida in brightly coloured wool.

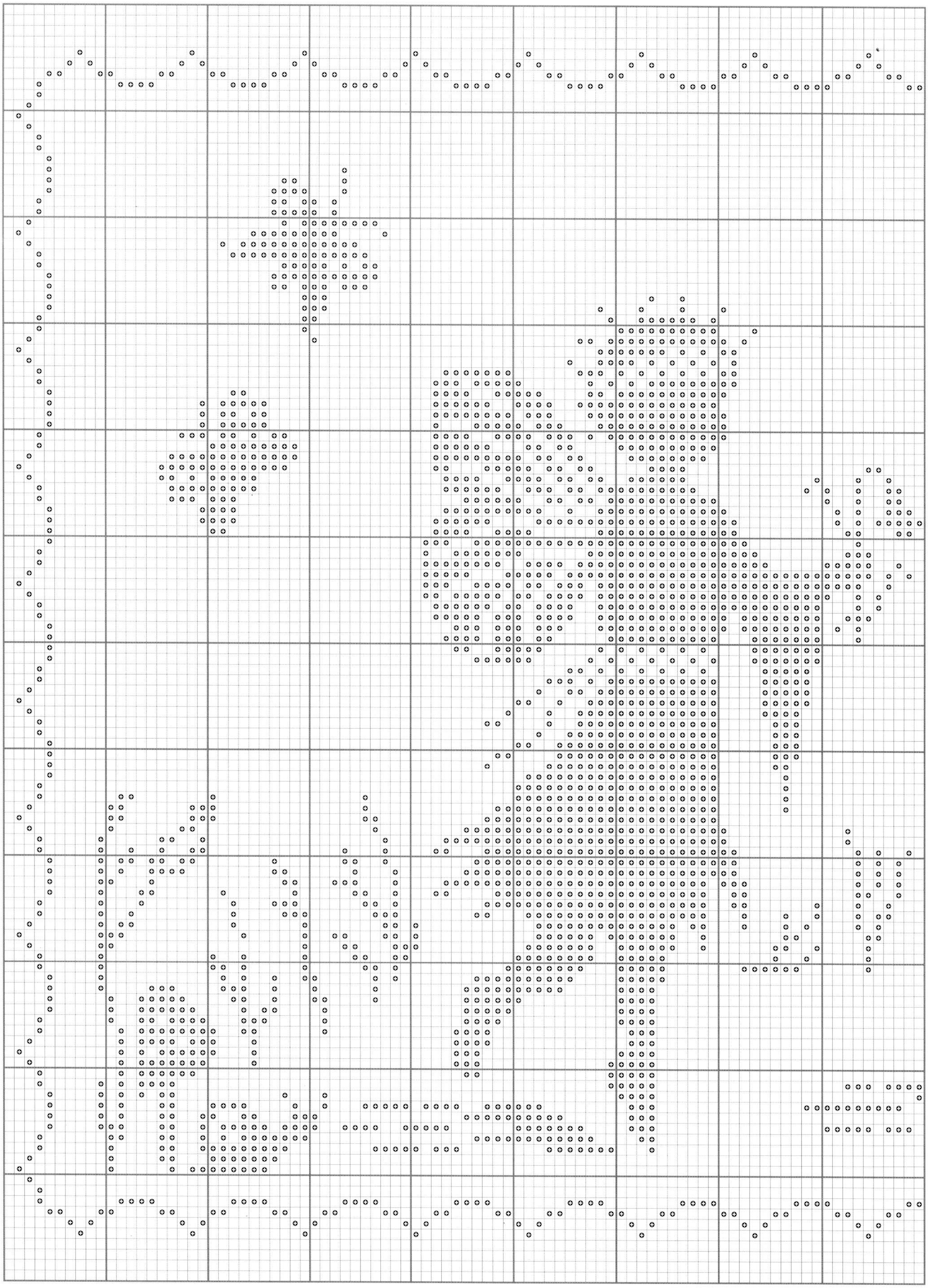

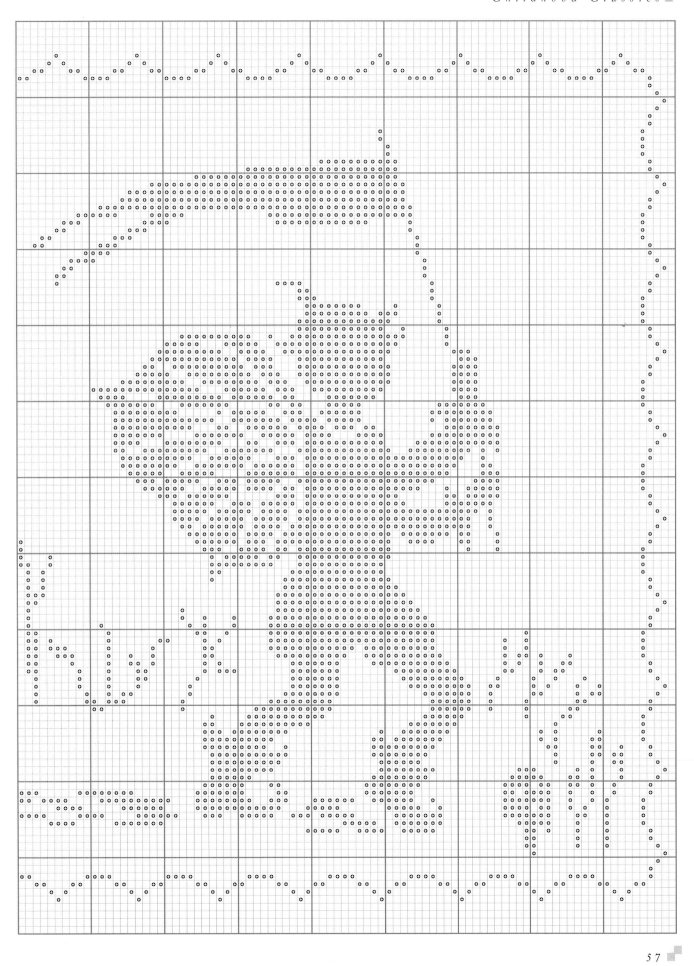

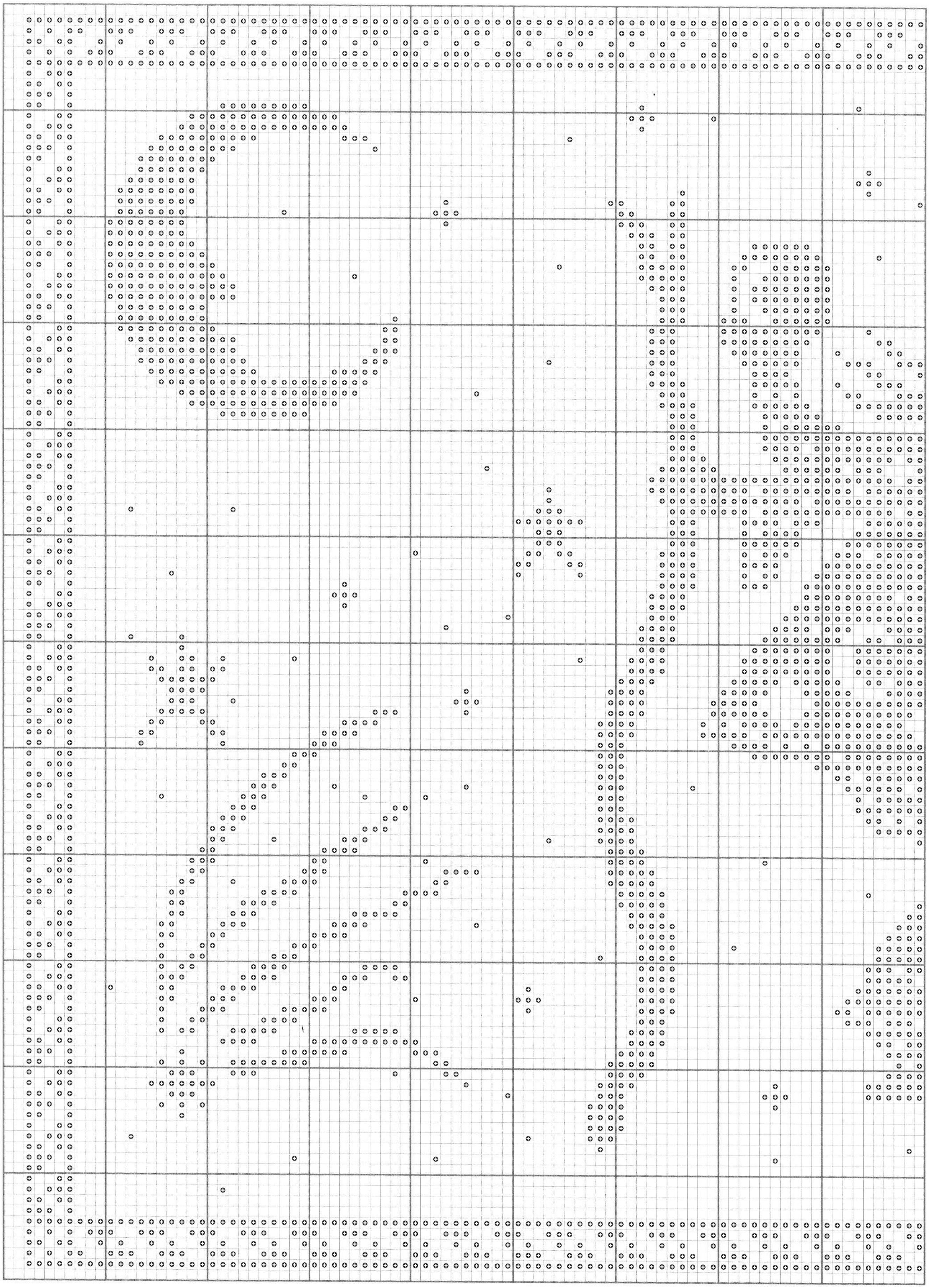

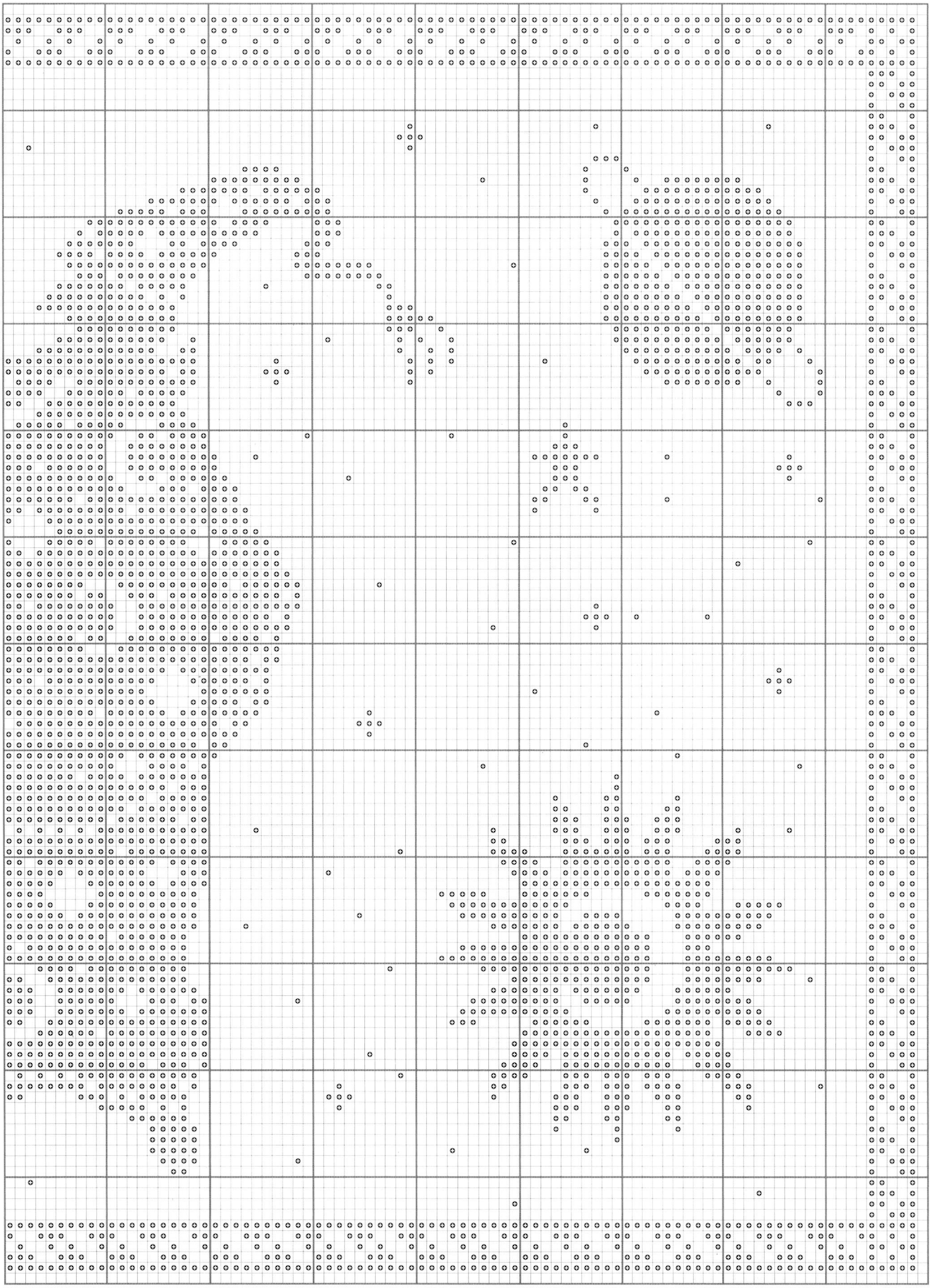

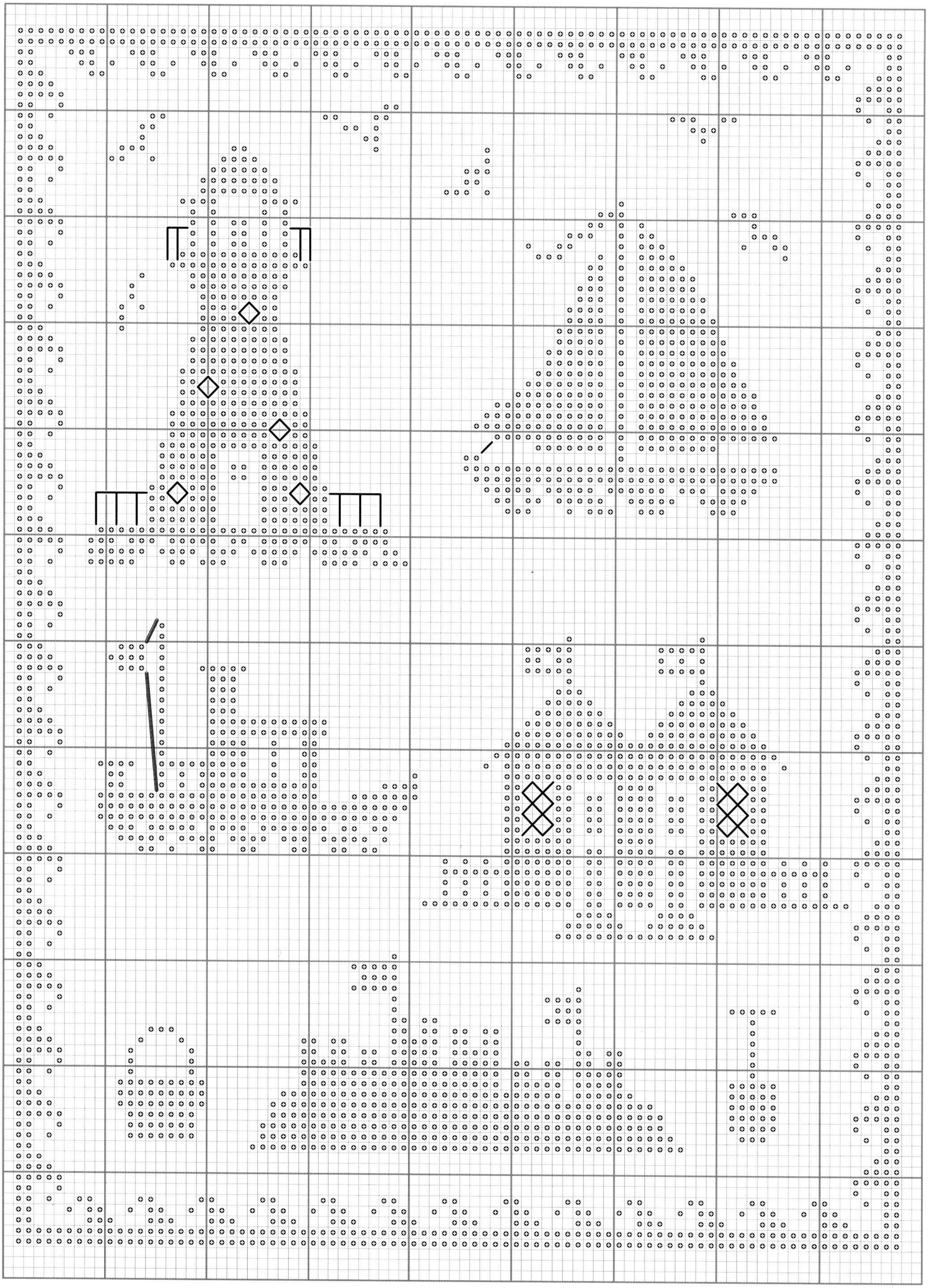

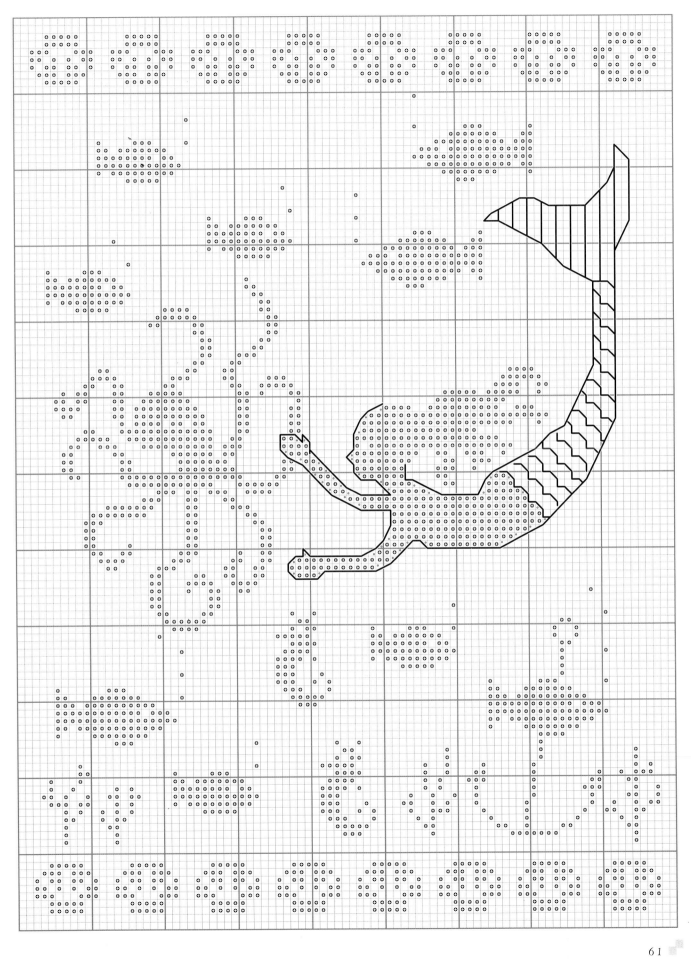

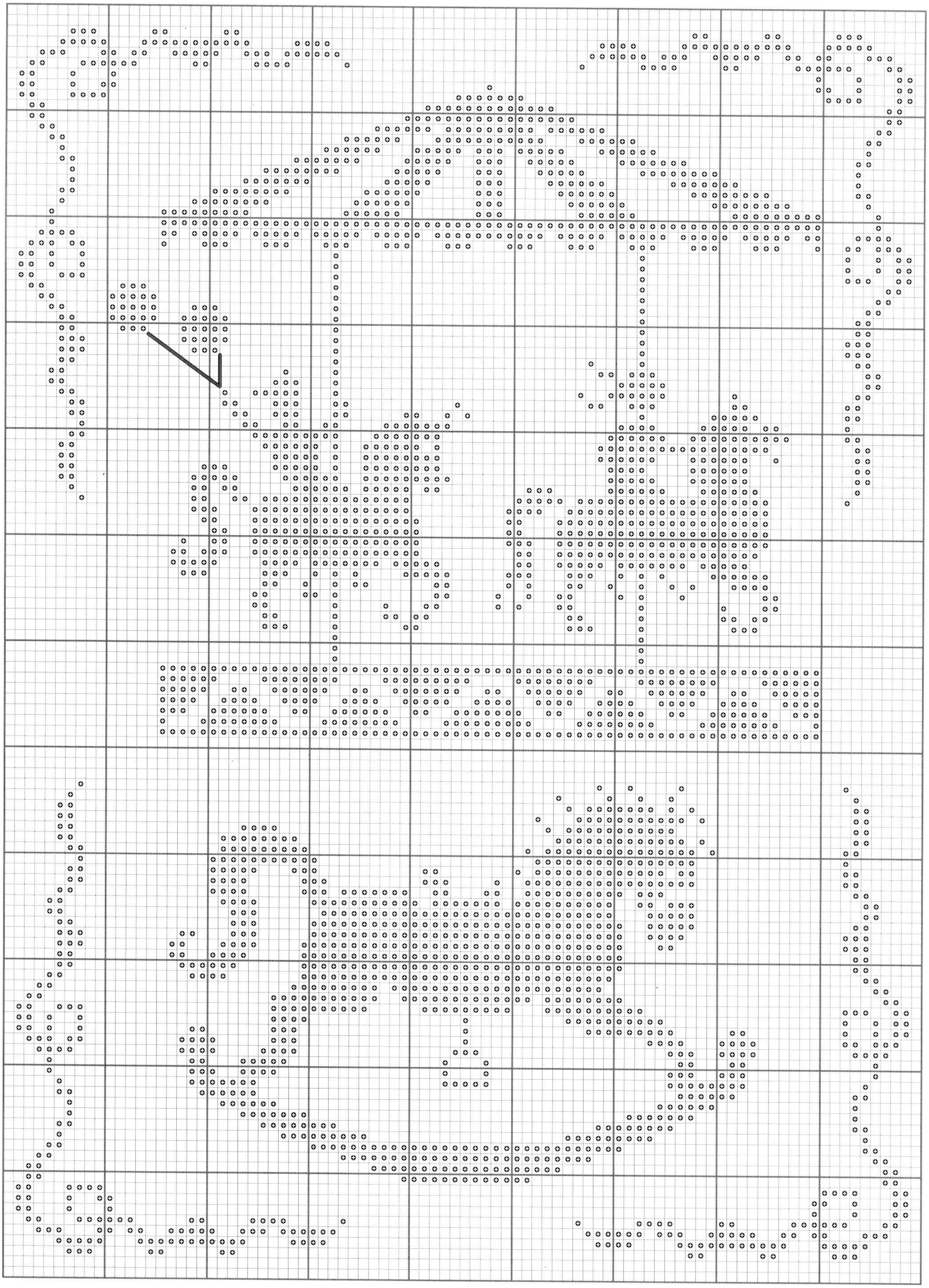

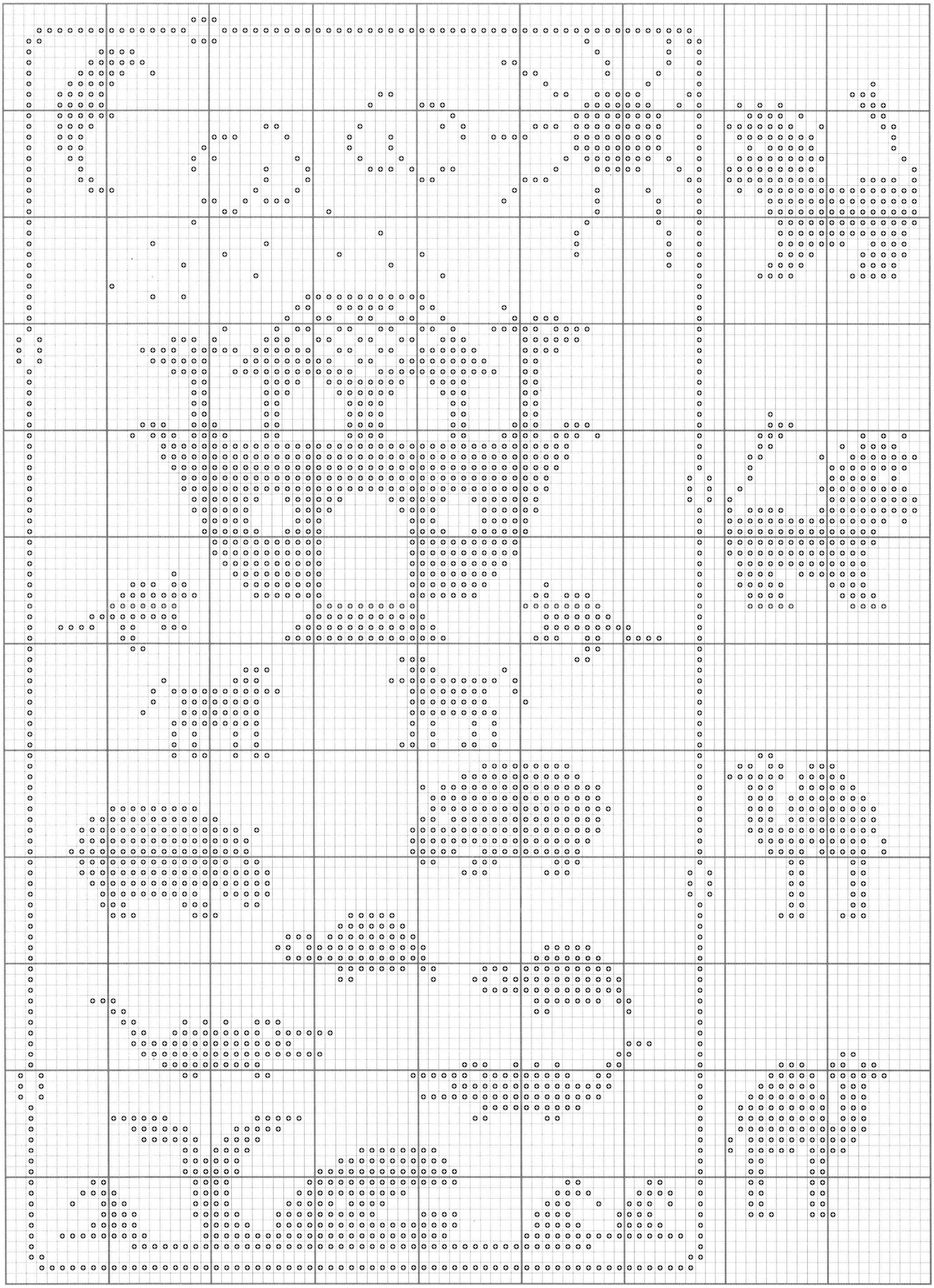

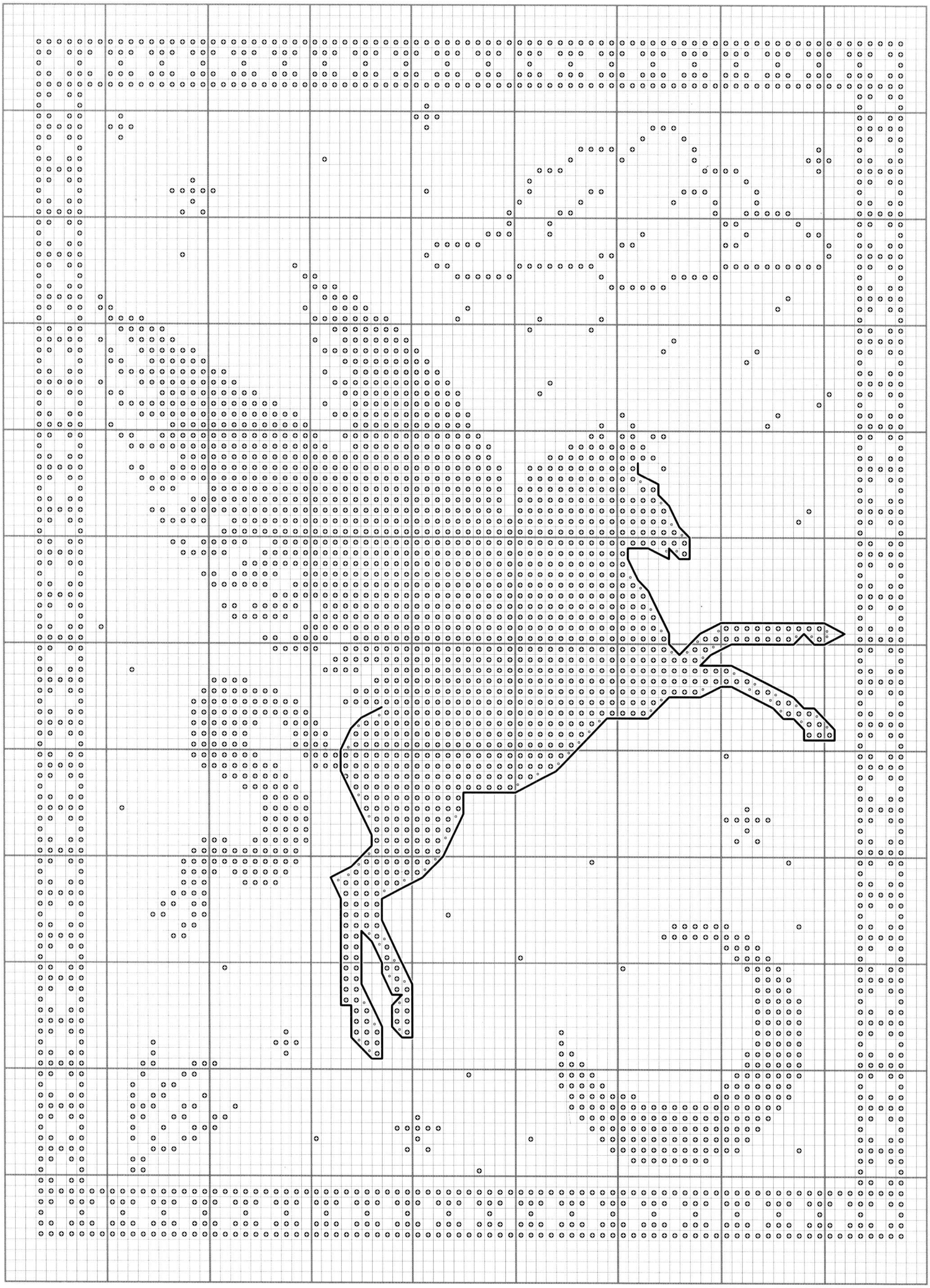

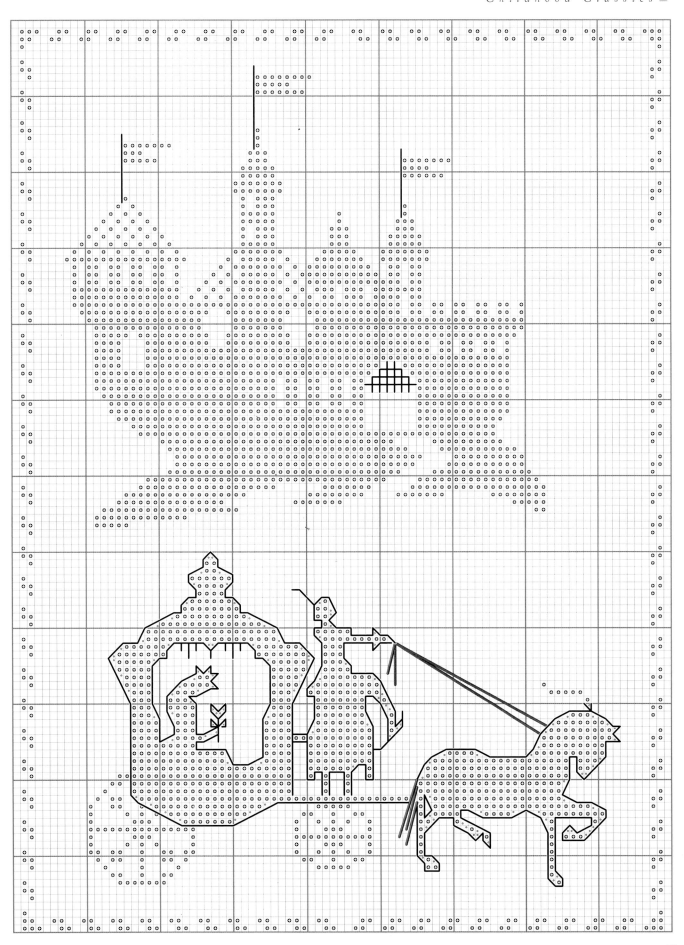

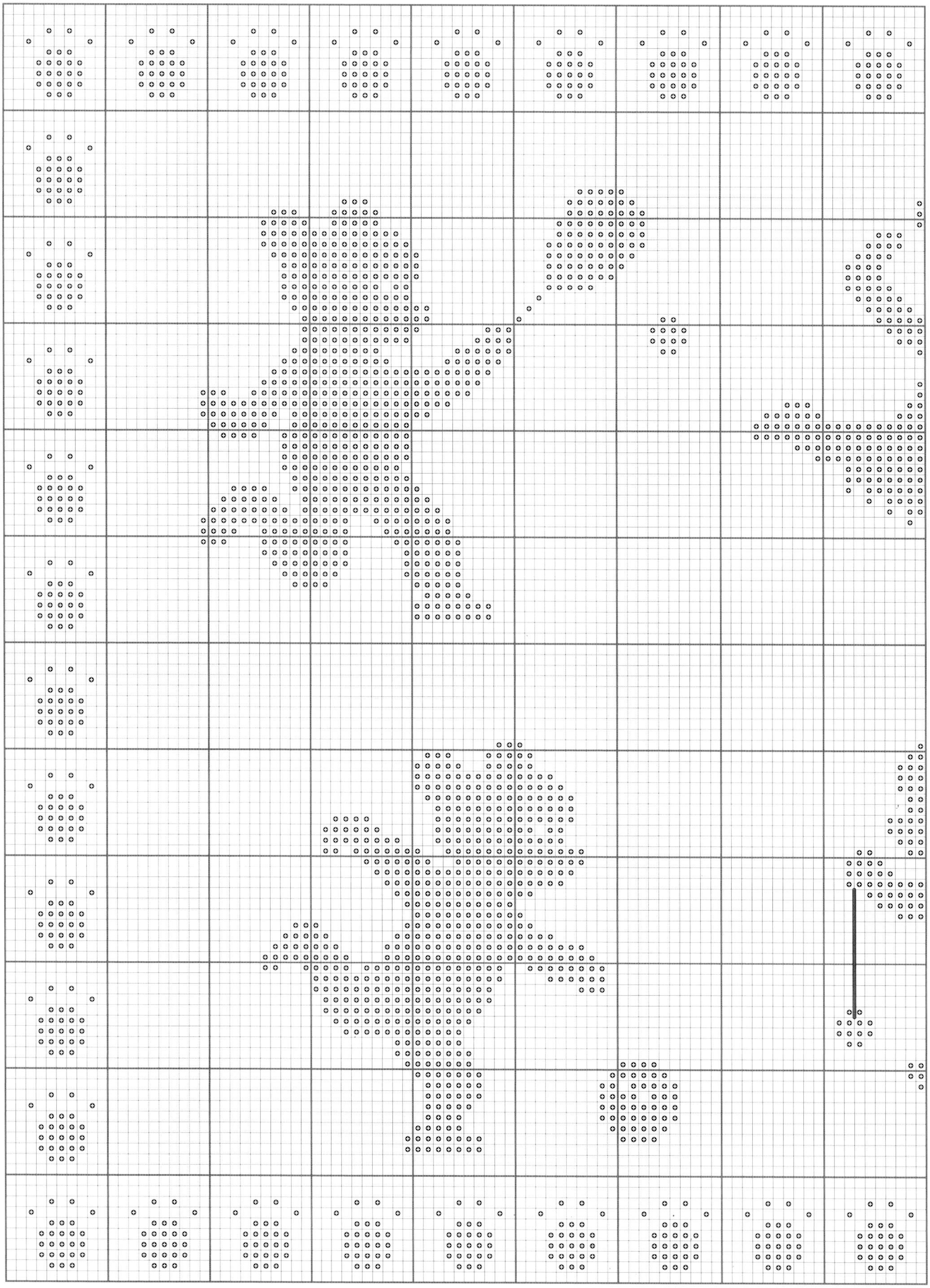

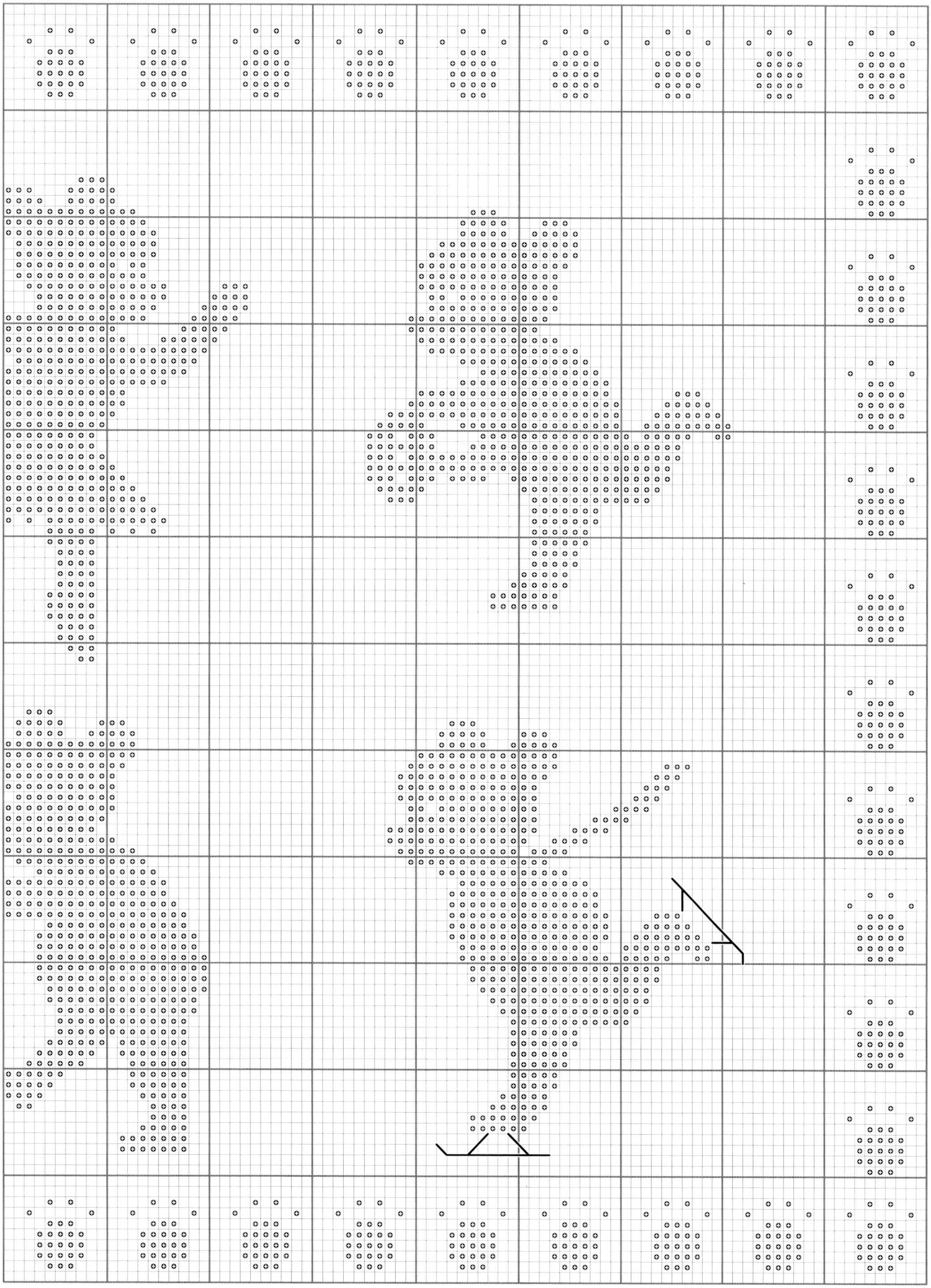

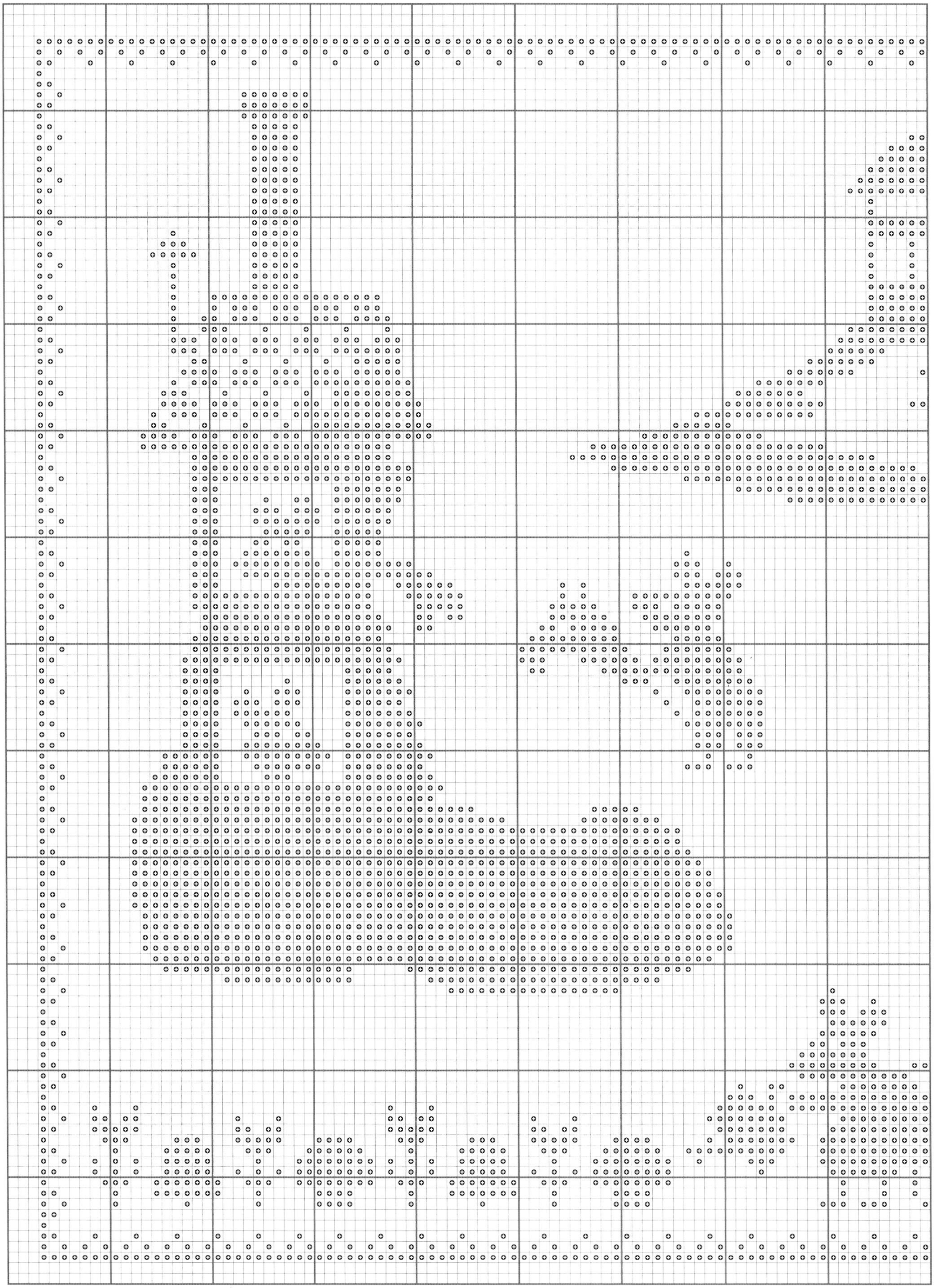

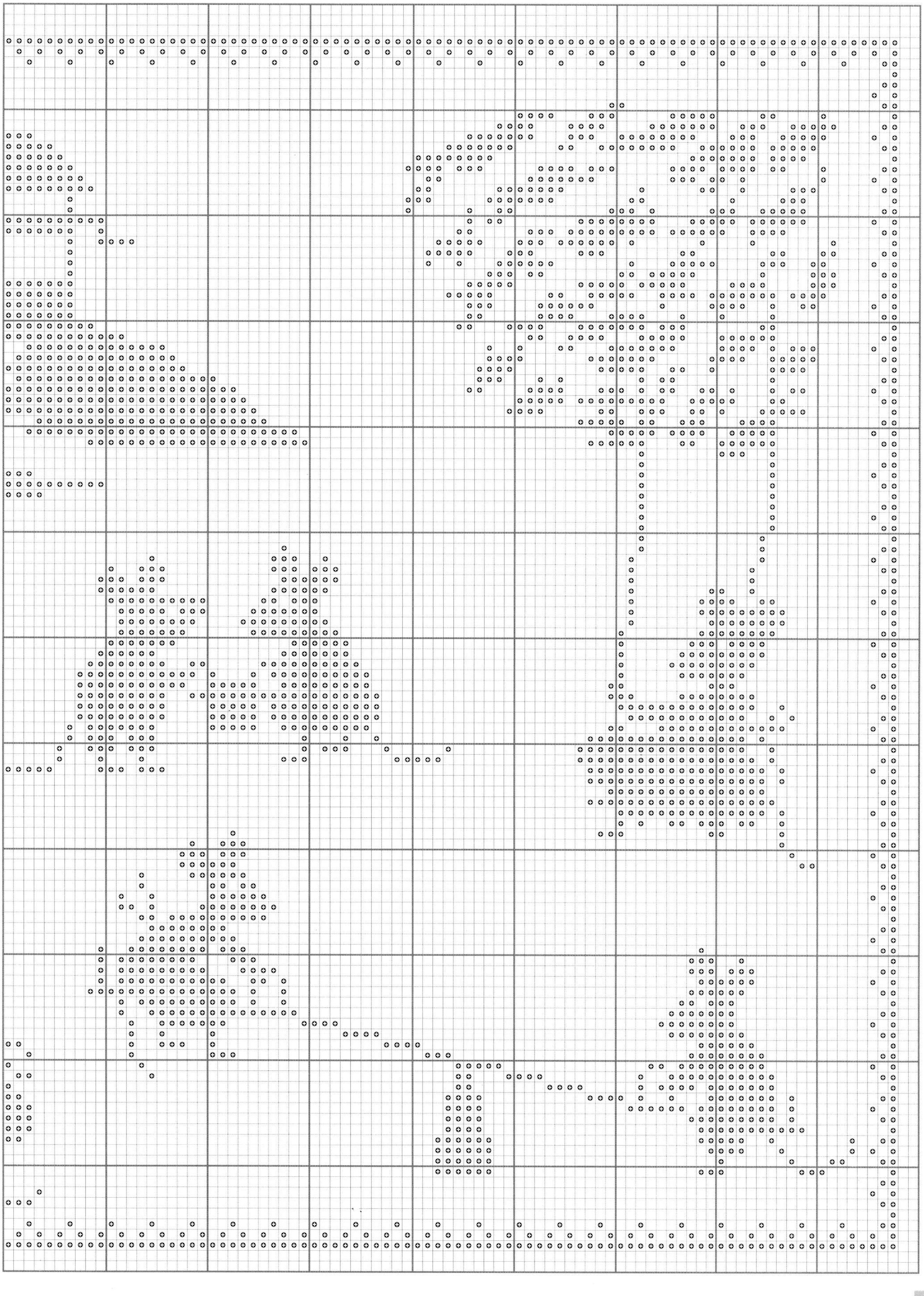

AROUND THE WORLD

T HE EXCITING DESIGNS in this chapter are of well-known sights, architecture and animals from far-flung places all around the world. They capture the colours and moods of the continents – the sunburnt plains of Africa, vibrant cosmopolitan cities, ancient civilisations and the serene beauty of the Orient. The Jobelan fabric used on items shown is a 28 count. When making up projects refer to Finishing and Making Up.

x x x x x x *Stitching notes* x x x x x x

Rest and relax with a travel pillow featuring safari animals stitched with two strands of dark grey stranded cotton on cream Jobelan. Your sunglasses or spectacles will be safe in a glasses case (from Framecraft) with a dream catcher stitched in silver grey on black 18 count Aida. Planning journeys is made easier with an itinerary diary. Inspired by the rich colours of the Orient, the pagoda is stitched with two strands of red stranded cotton on black Jobelan. The diary can either be covered in contrasting fabric and the embroidery slipstitched into position, or the stitched fabric alone can be used. A pretty trinket roll (see page 124) made from light blue Jobelan fabric forms the perfect backdrop for the timeless Taj Mahal stitched in silver grey. Inside, an elephant and lotus blossom add to the romance of India. A small treasure chest is the ideal place to keep souvenirs or excess holiday money. The box with a padded lid is from Framecraft and features majestic pyramids stitched in dark grey on forget-me-not blue Jobelan fabric.

x x x x x x x x x x x x x x x x x x x x x x

VARIATIONS ON A THEME

■ Stitch the romantic Eiffel Tower bookmark on dark blue fabric with silver thread. A tote bag stitched with a scene from the South Seas in blue would make a great beach bag. Create a dramatic picture of an American Indian scene in cross stitch on cream fabric, stitching the tepee in stone coloured thread and the brave and totem pole in dark brown.

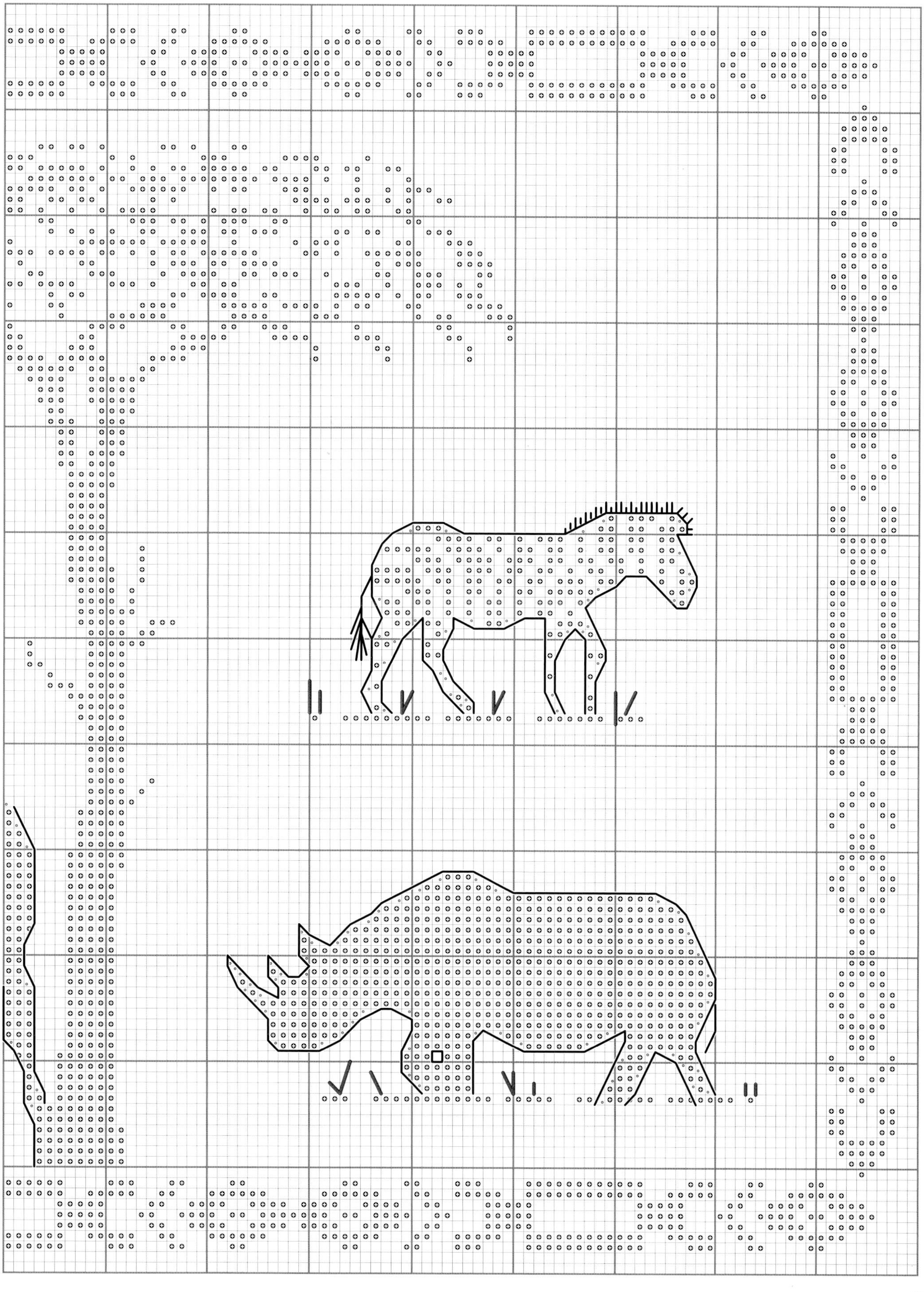

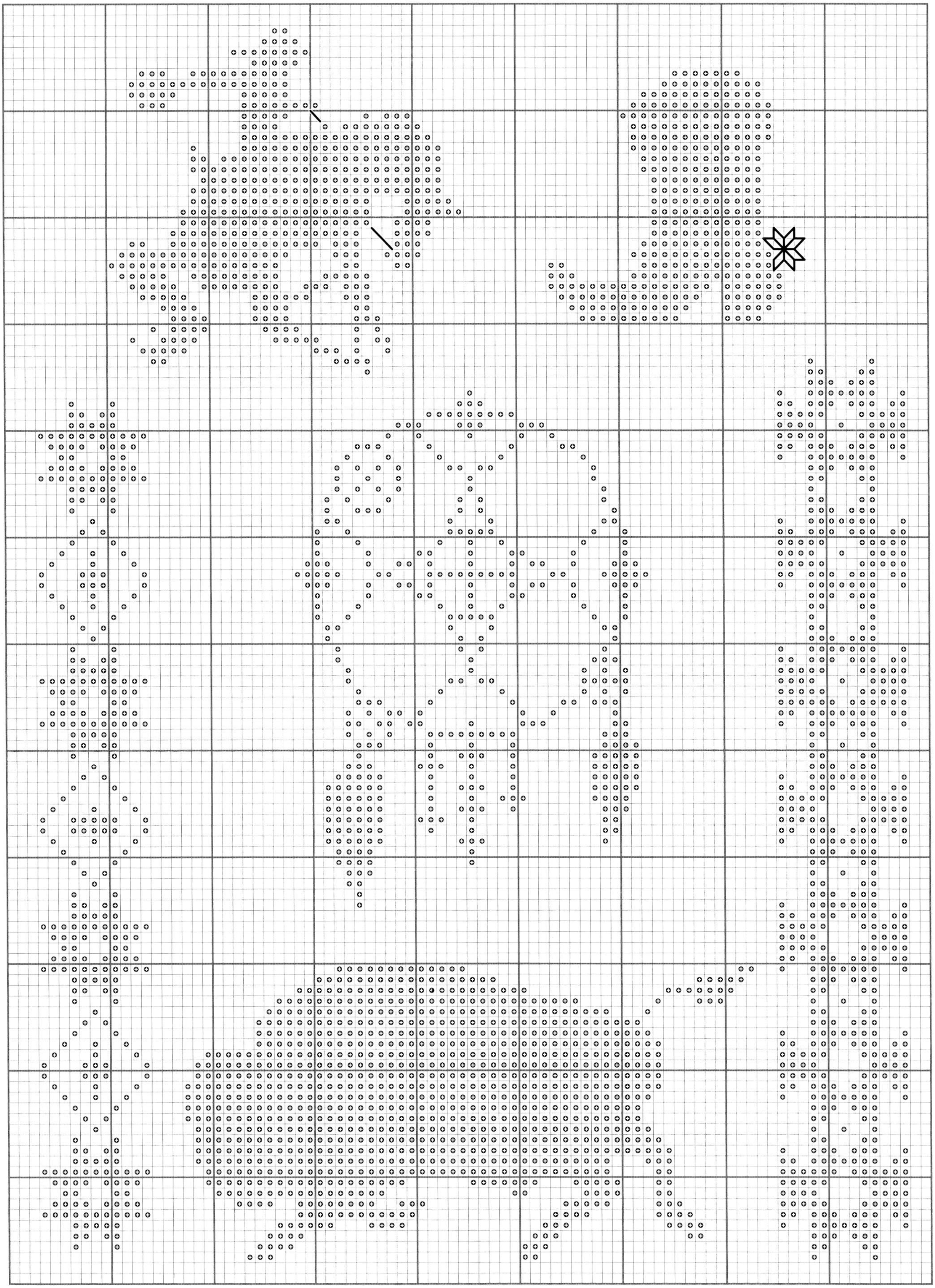

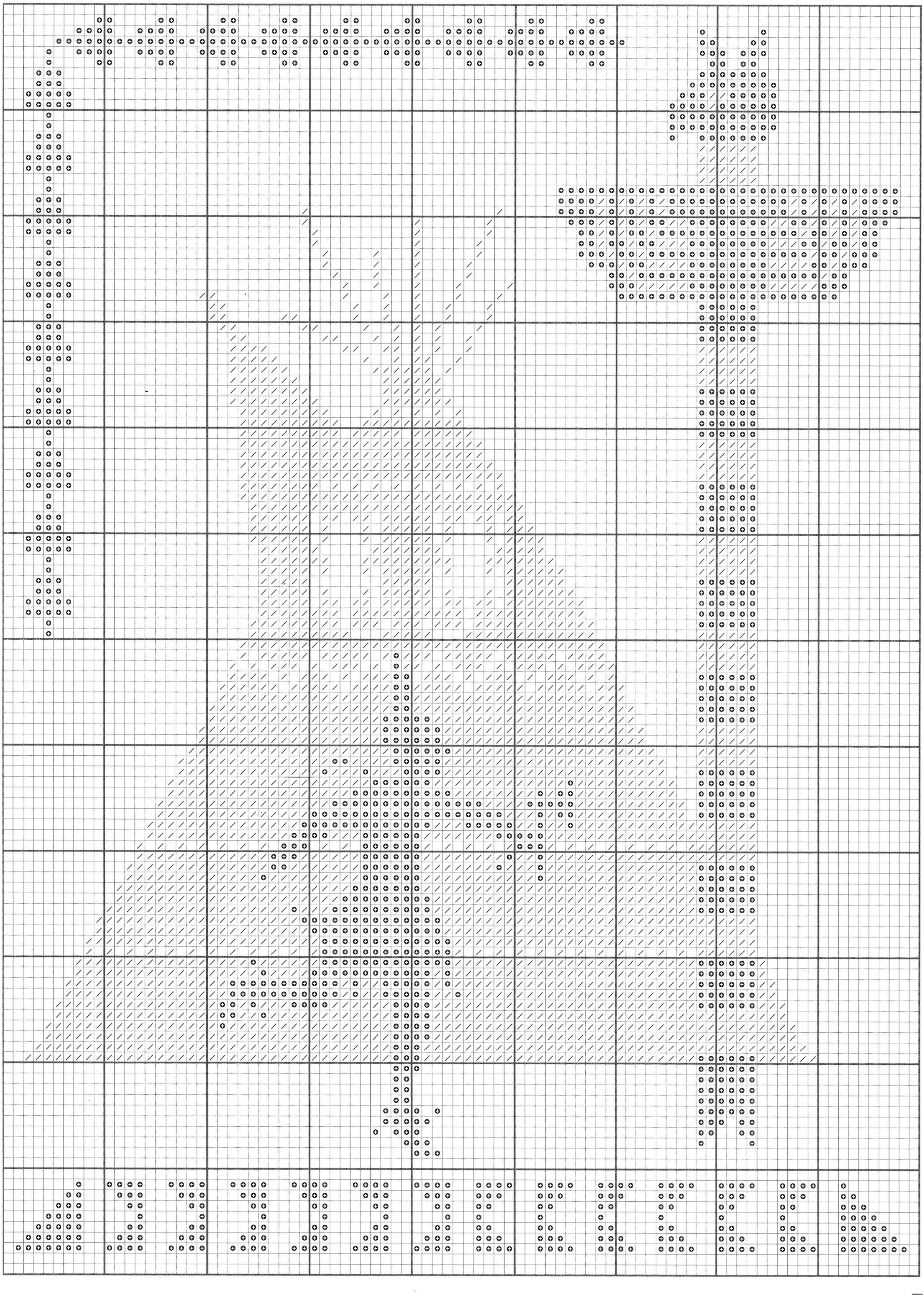

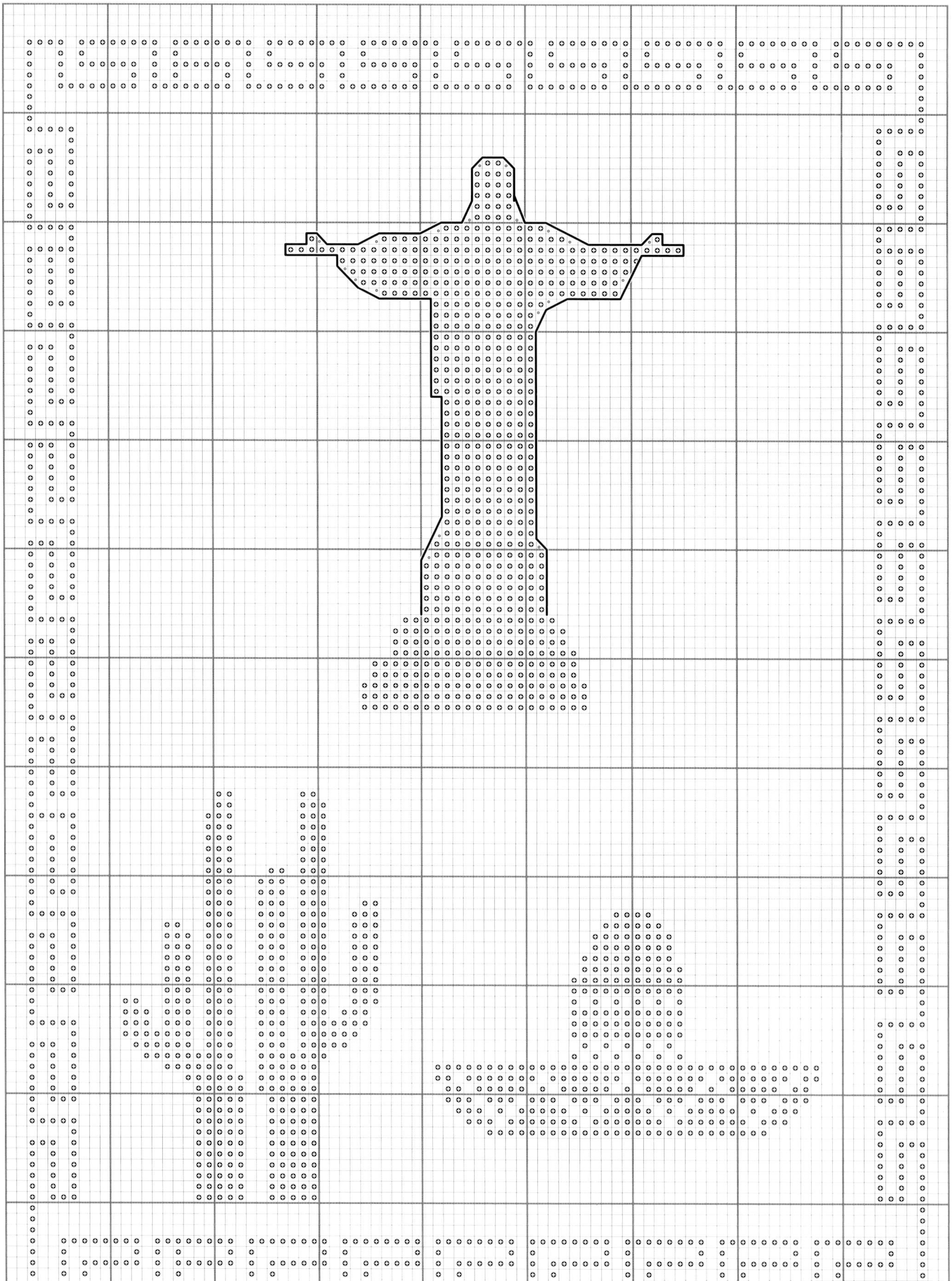

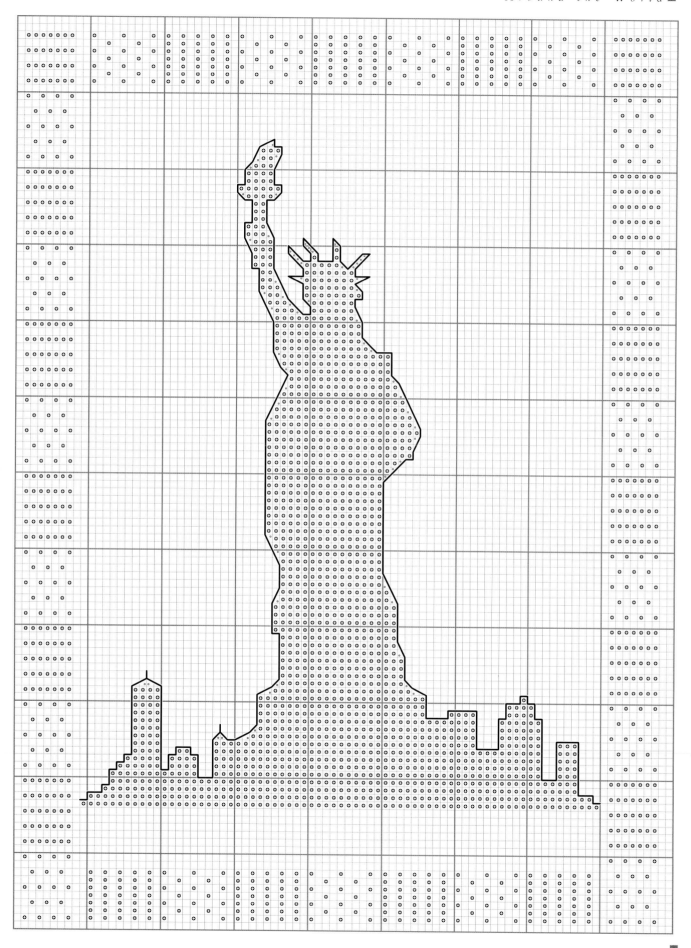

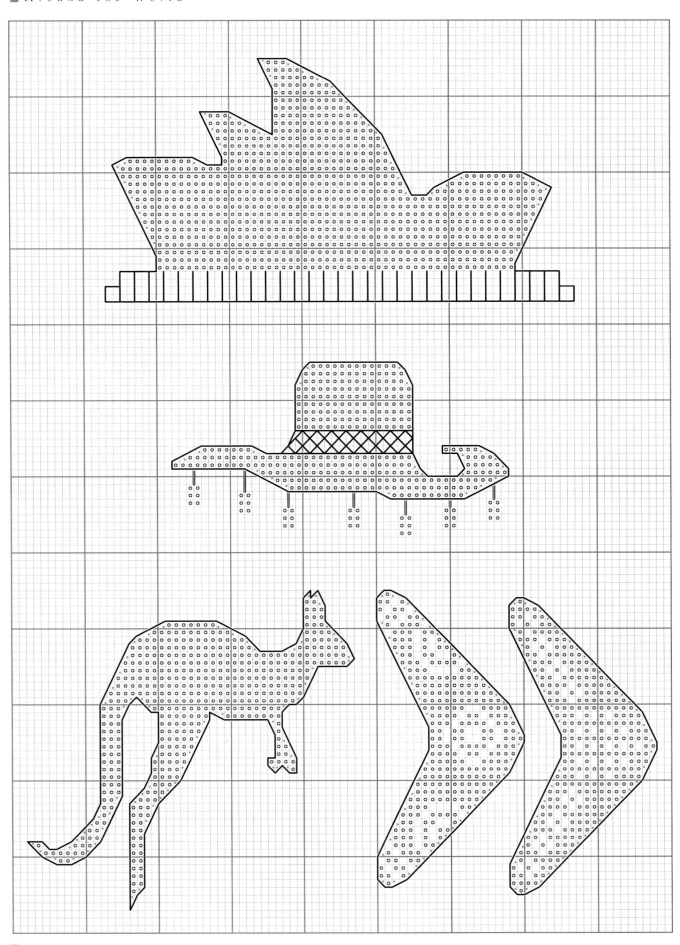

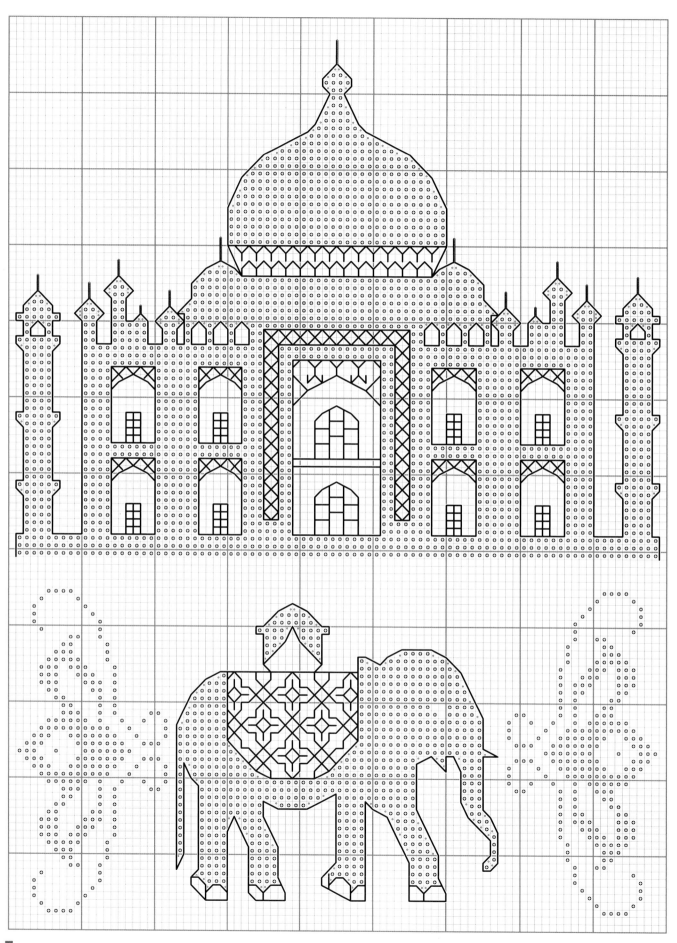

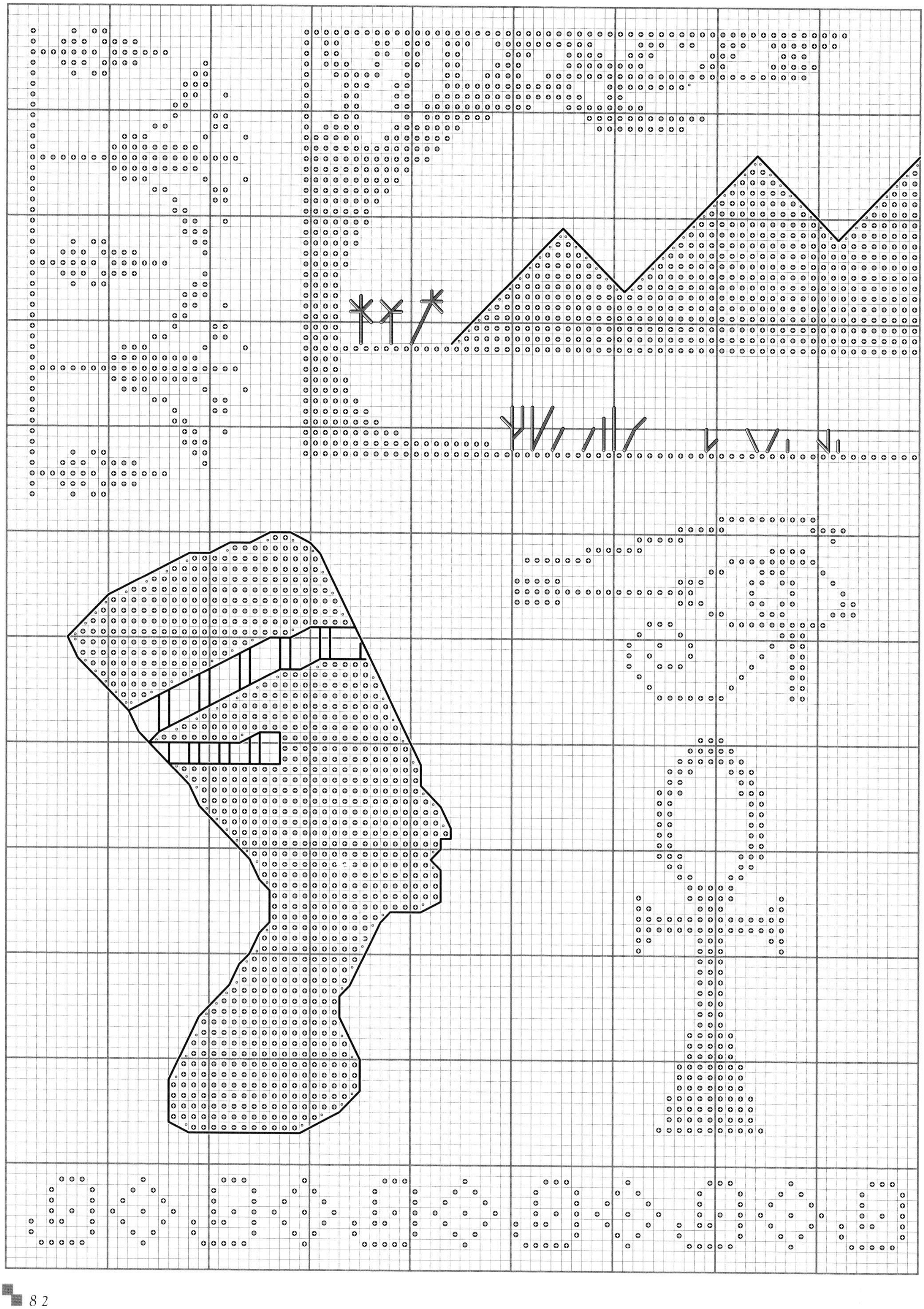

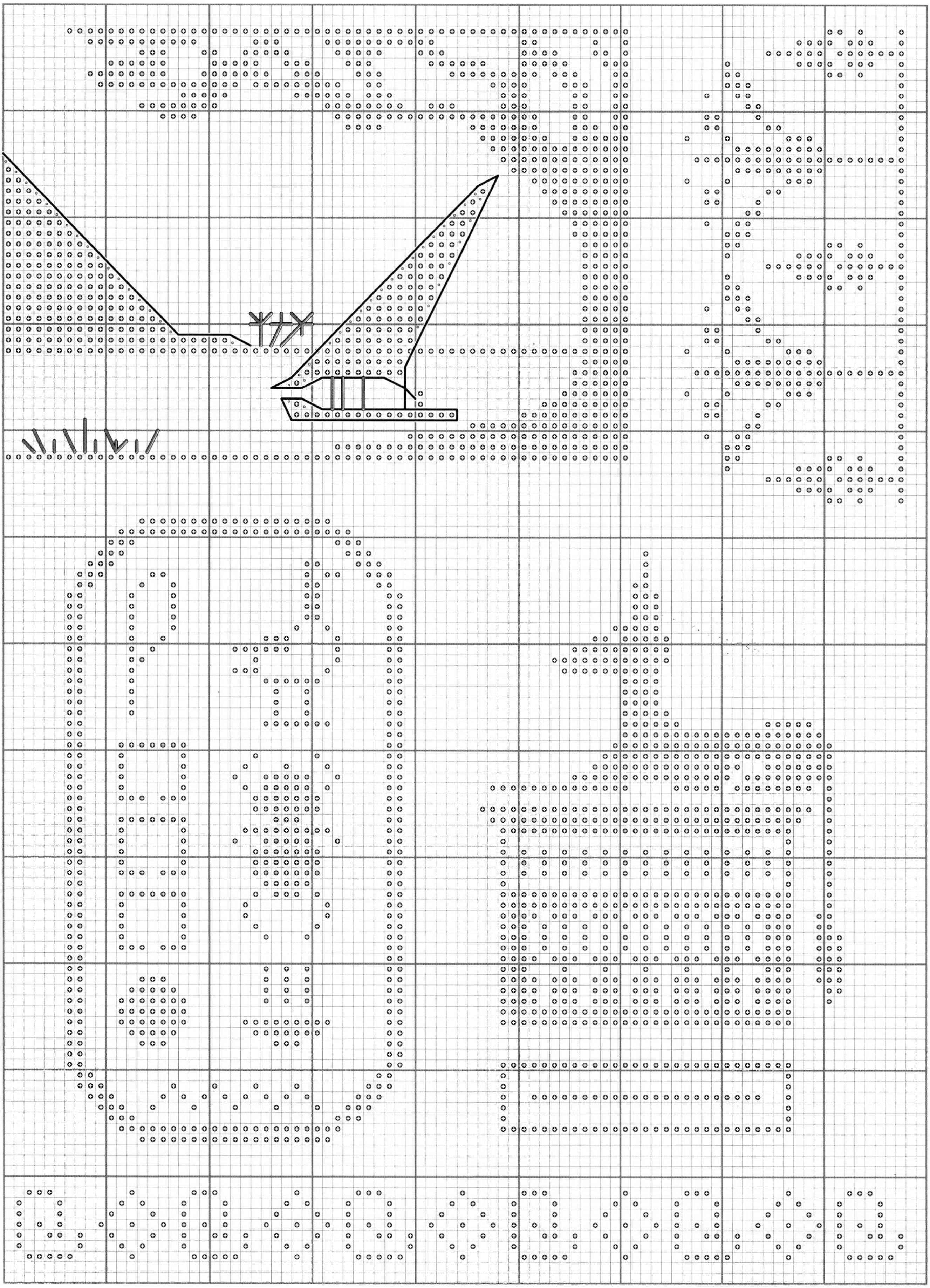

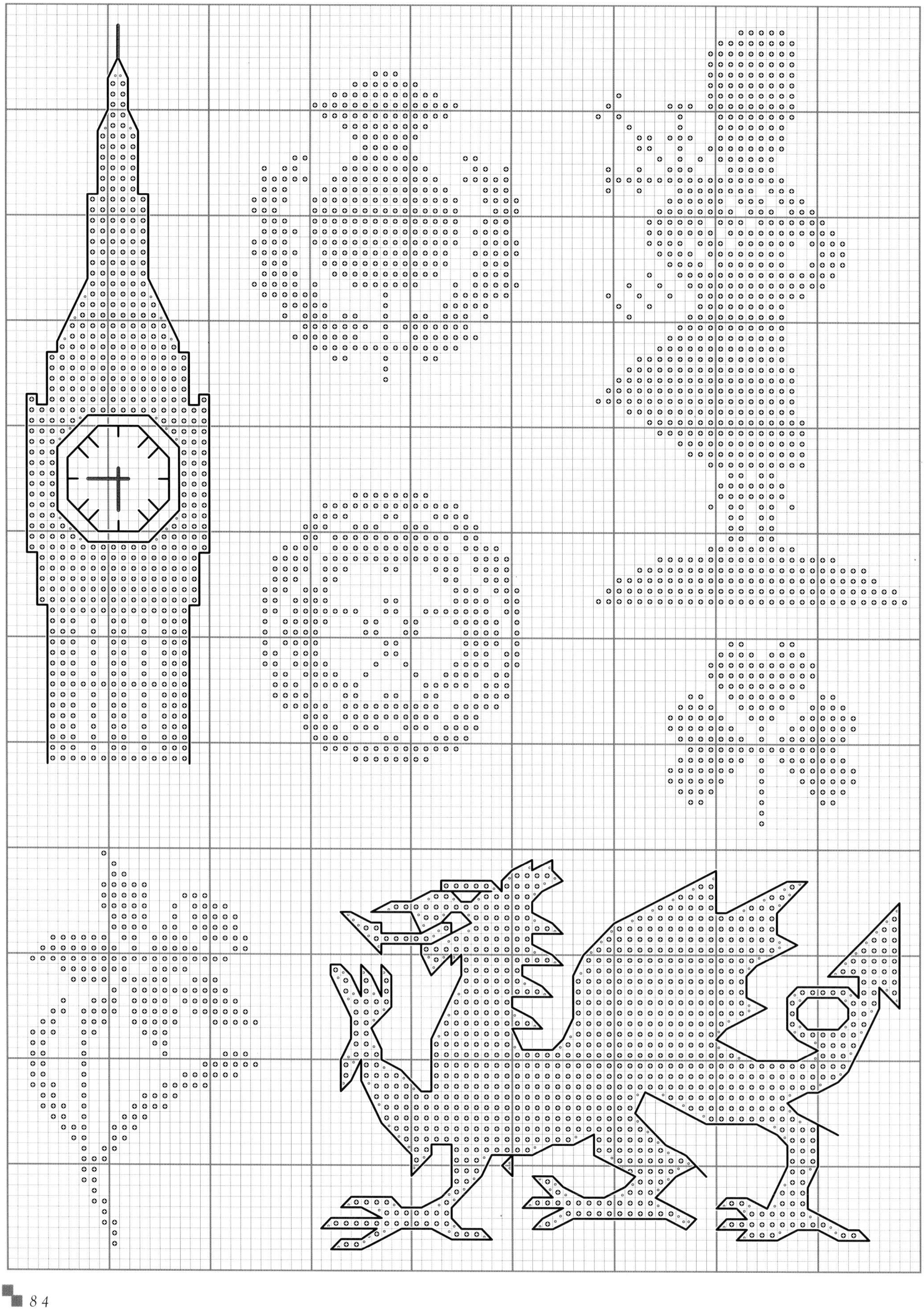

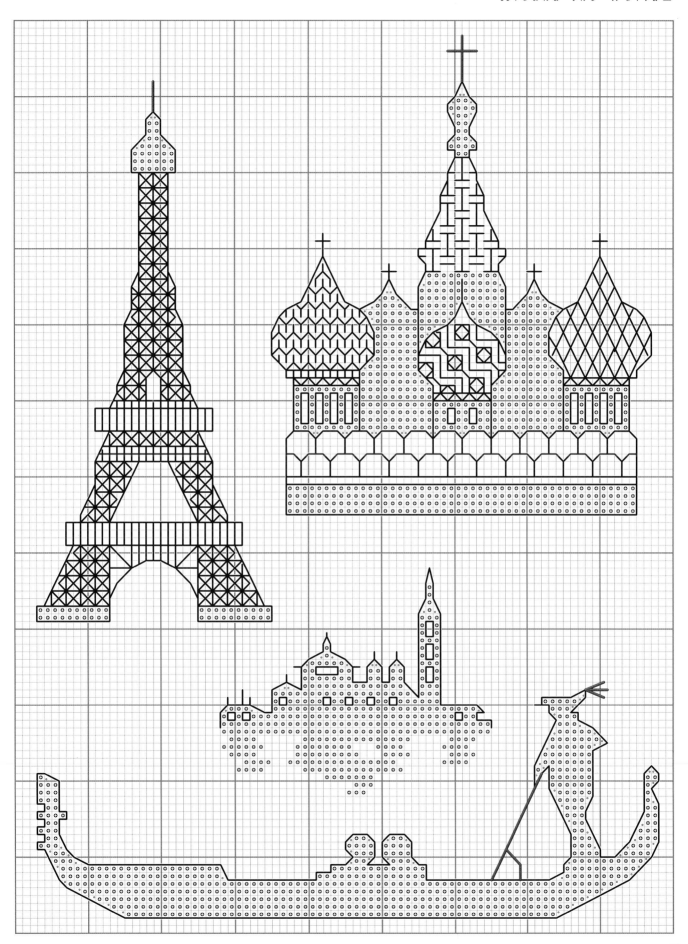

CELEBRATIONS

HIS CHAPTER has literally dozens of celebratory motifs to suit all of life's special events. There are designs to celebrate births, Christenings, birthdays, engagements, weddings and anniversaries. There are images to reflect life's successes – hearts, flowers, bells, keys, champagne and lucky horseshoes, and special days such as Easter, Thanksgiving, Hallowe'en, fireworks night and much more. When making up projects refer to Finishing and Making Up.

× × × × × × *Stitching notes* × × × × × × ×

A bridal trousseau would be complemented by this beautiful wedding ring cushion stitched with two strands of a golden yellow rayon thread over two threads of ivory white 28 count linen. It has been edged with cotton lace, together with yellow and white ribbons. The birth of a baby is also a very special occasion and to mark the event cute yellow ducks have been stitched with two strands of stranded cotton onto 14 count white baby booties from Framecraft. A ruby coloured Raj Mahal box from Fabric Flair makes a lovely gift for a special birthday or wedding anniversary. A heart-shaped motif has been stitched onto white 18 count Aida using a thread colour to match the box and the design has been adapted for a fortieth occasion, though the colour and number could be easily changed for a different anniversary.

× ×

VARIATIONS ON A THEME

■ The heart-shaped motif is a very adaptable design and could also be used with the initials of a person's name to make a special gift. An alarm clock design could be stitched as a retirement gift, using fabric and stranded cotton to suit the colour of a commercial clock casing. Stitch a key motif in a key-ring to celebrate the passing of a driving test, or the liner motif in a luggage label to wish bon voyage to someone going on a cruise. Stitch an 18 or 21 motif in a card for that special key-of-the-door birthday. Make a bag to feature one of the spooky Hallowe'en designs.

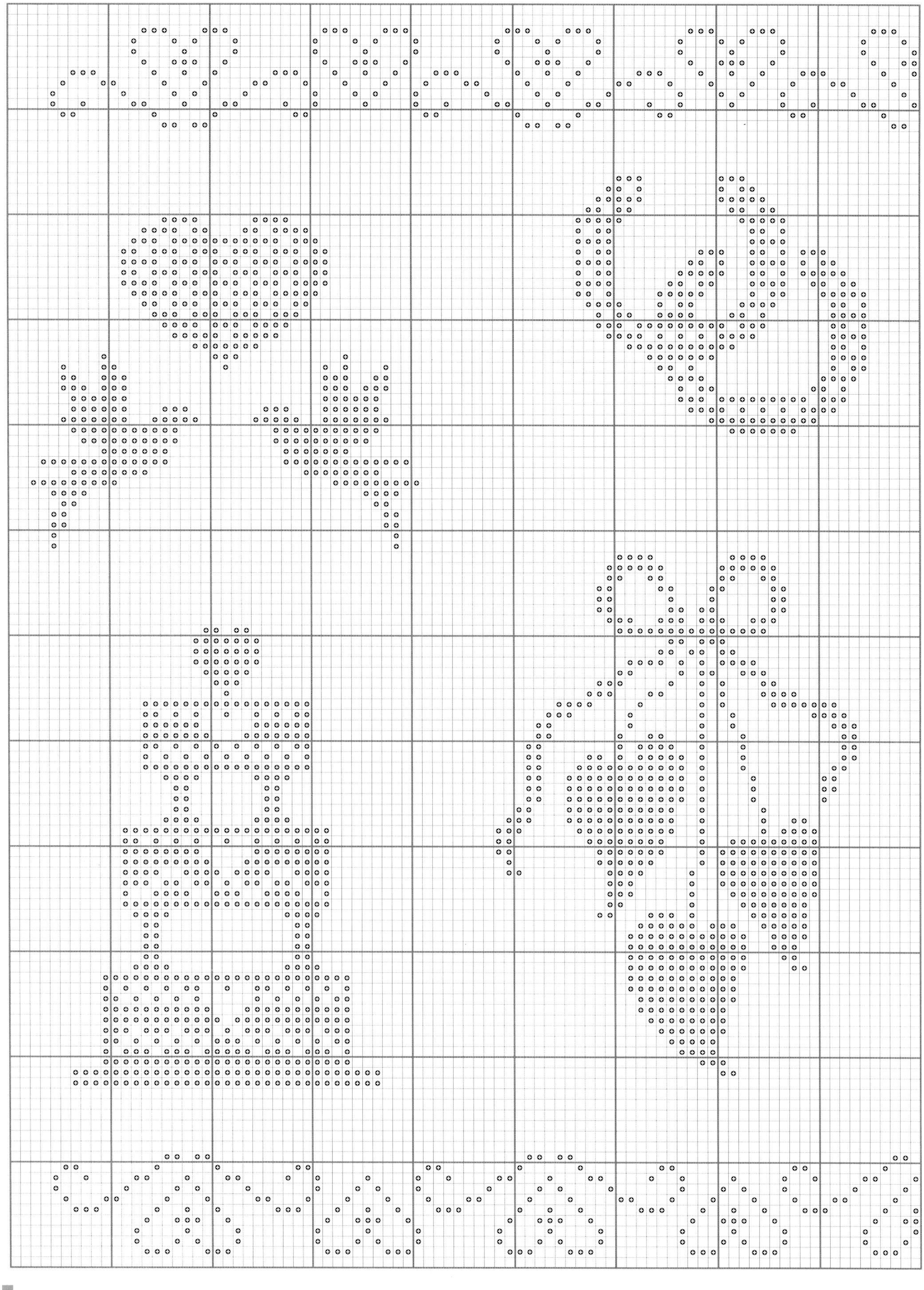

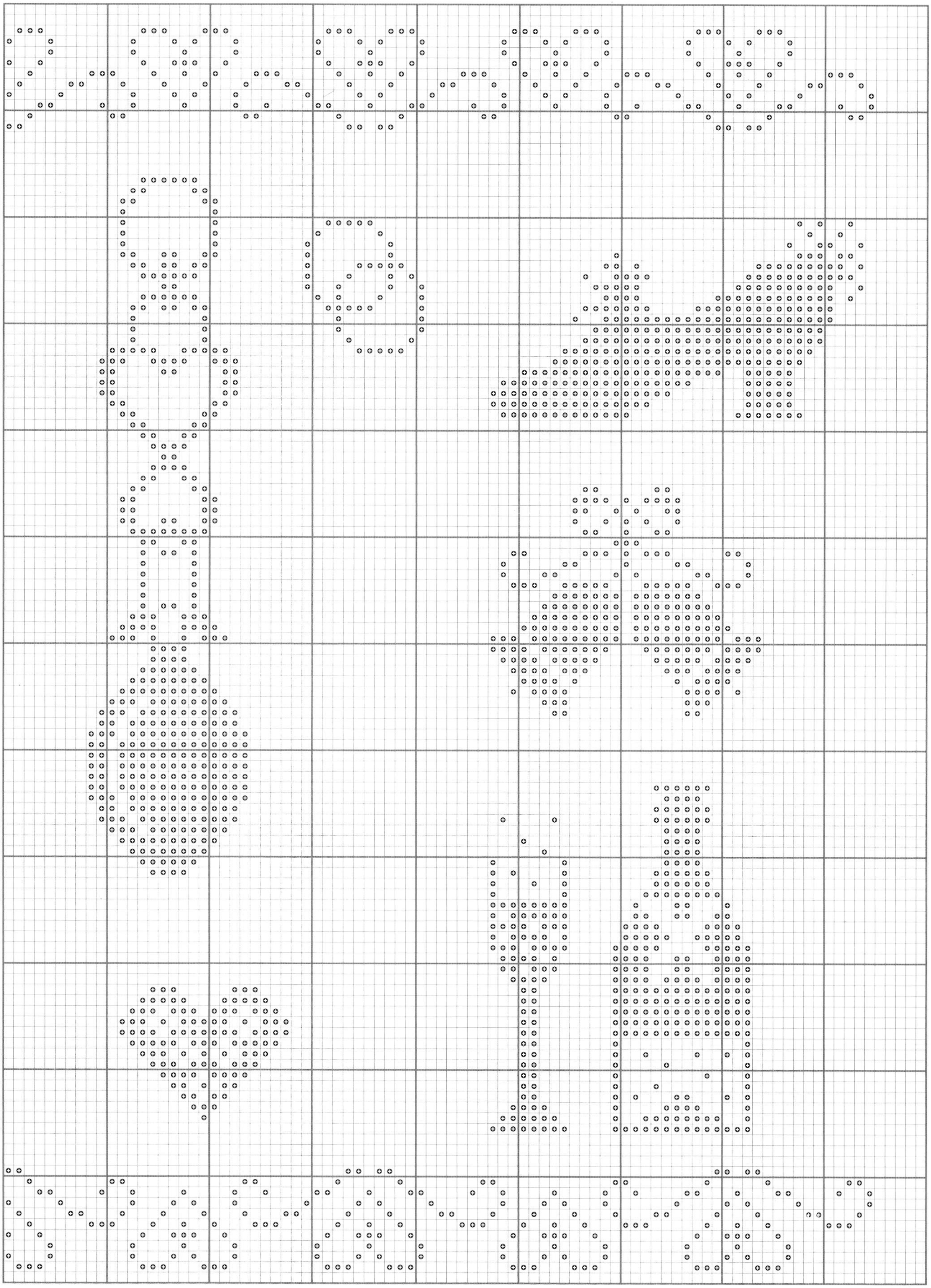

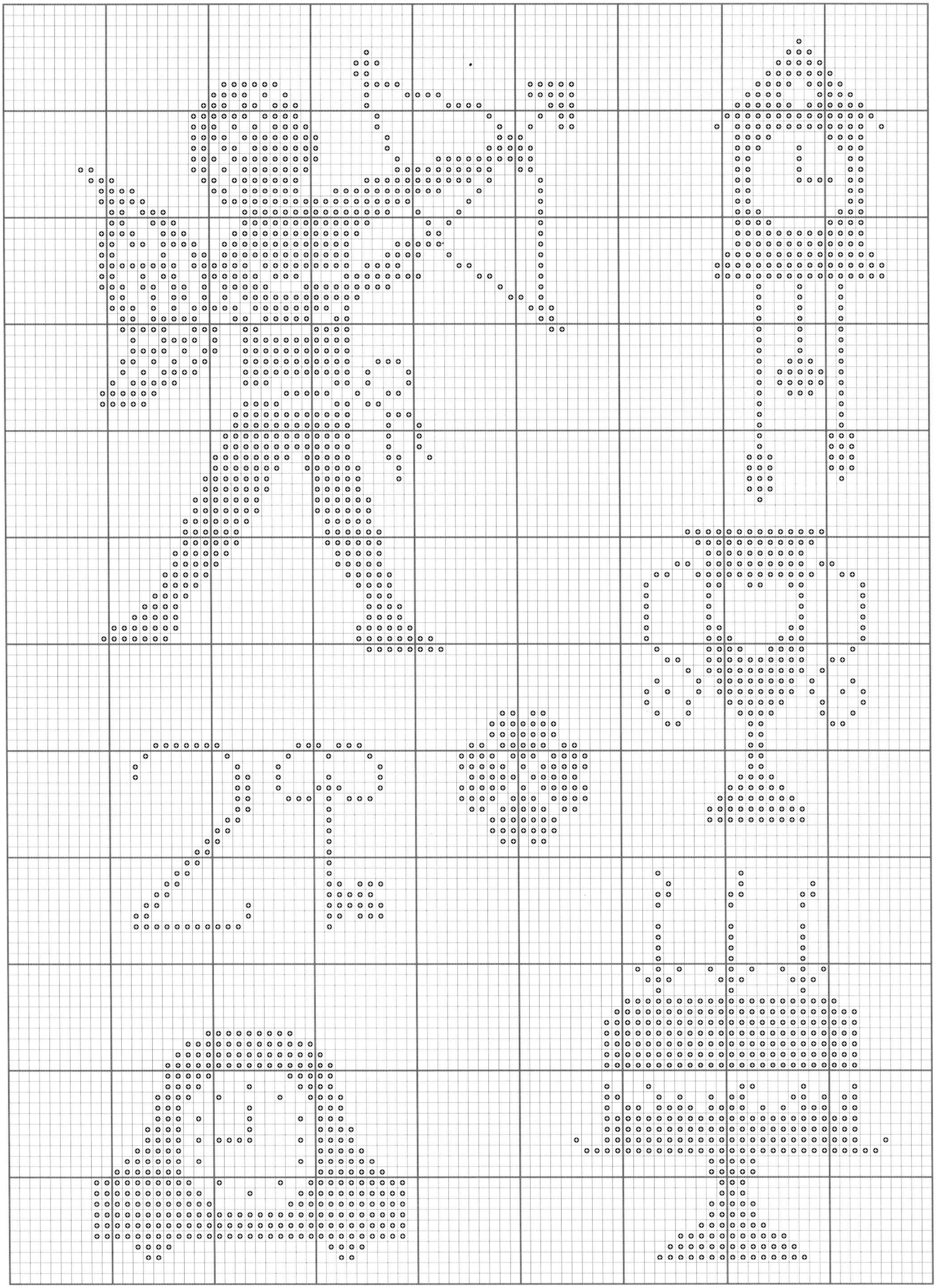

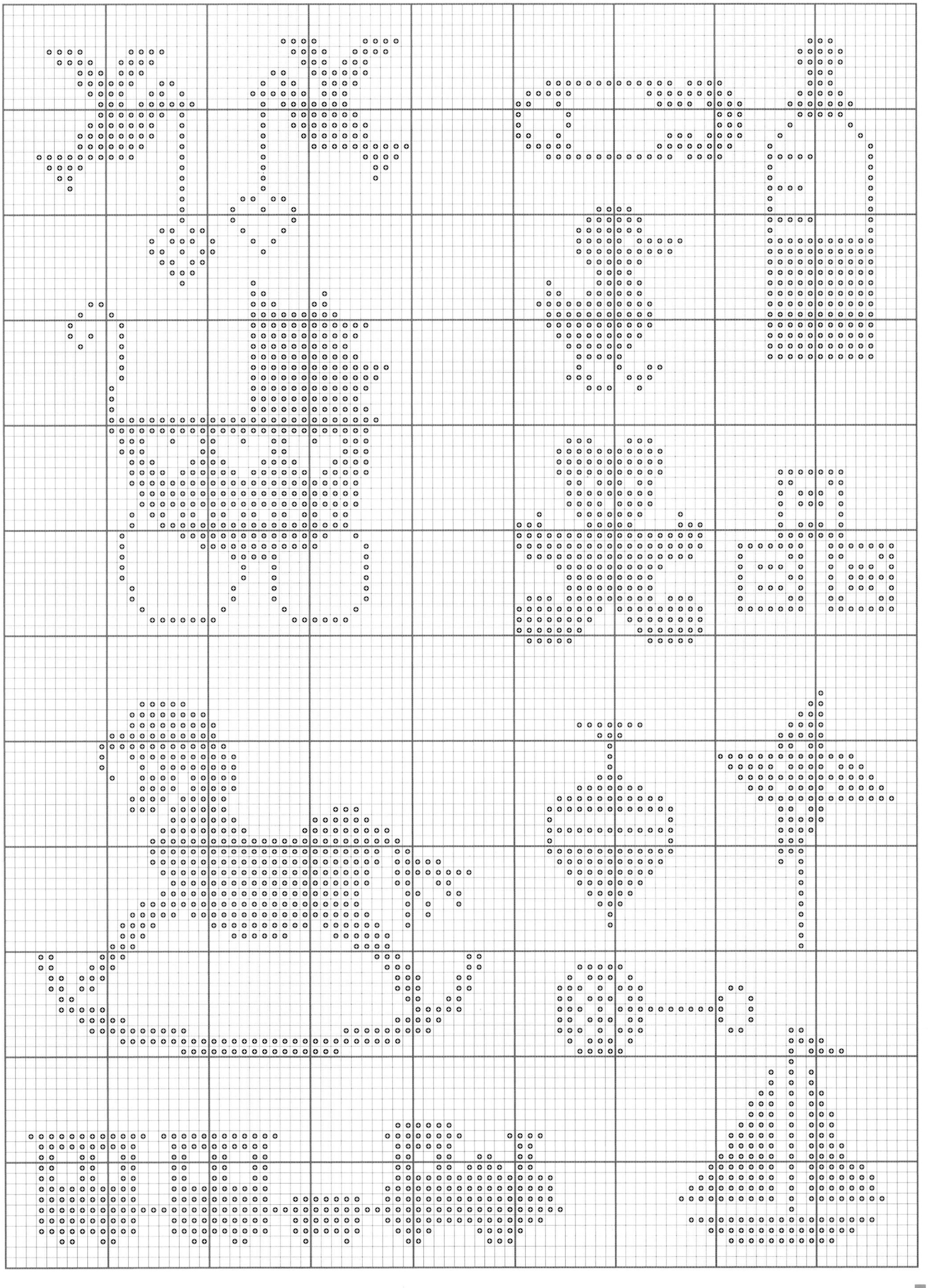

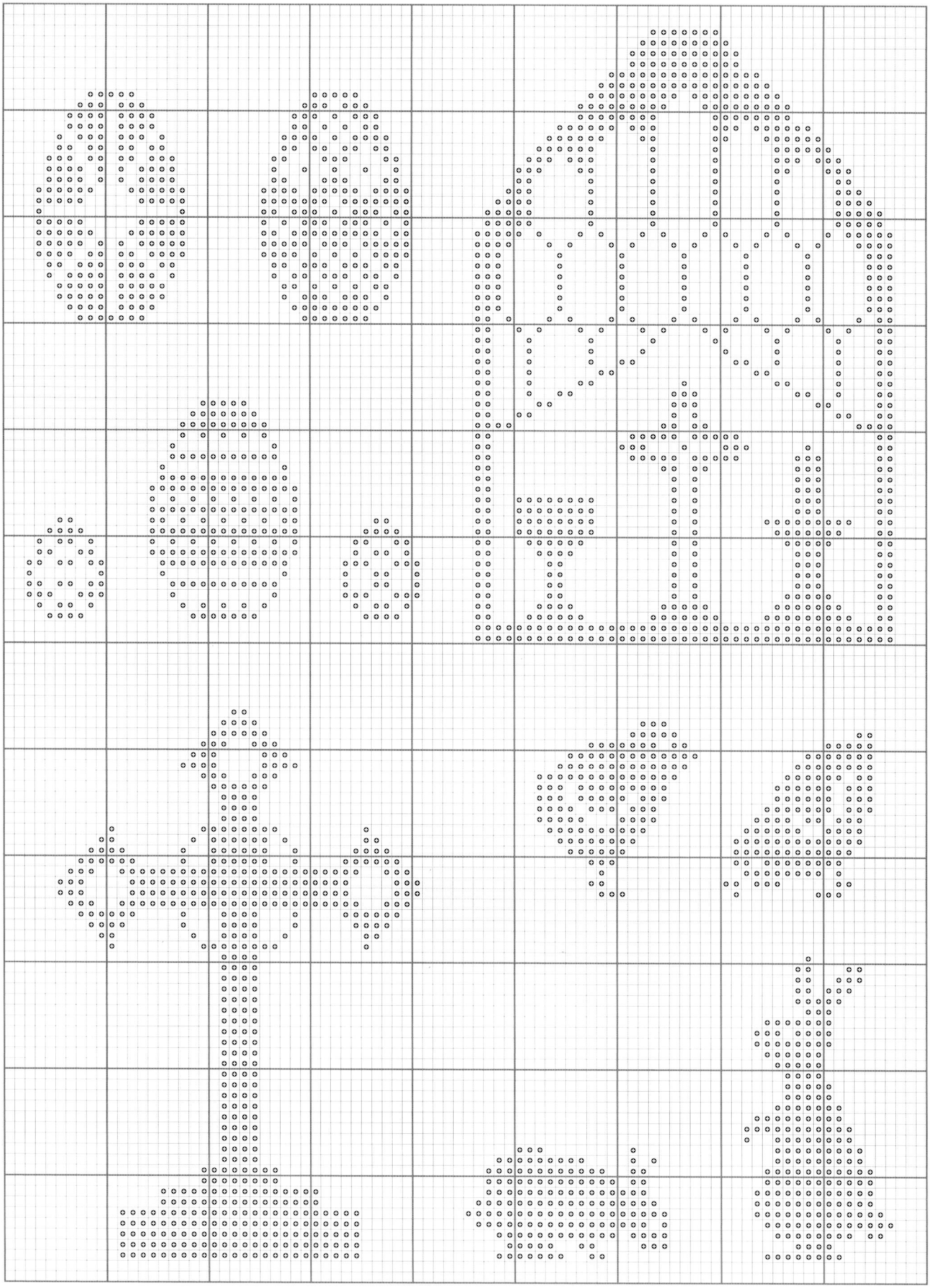

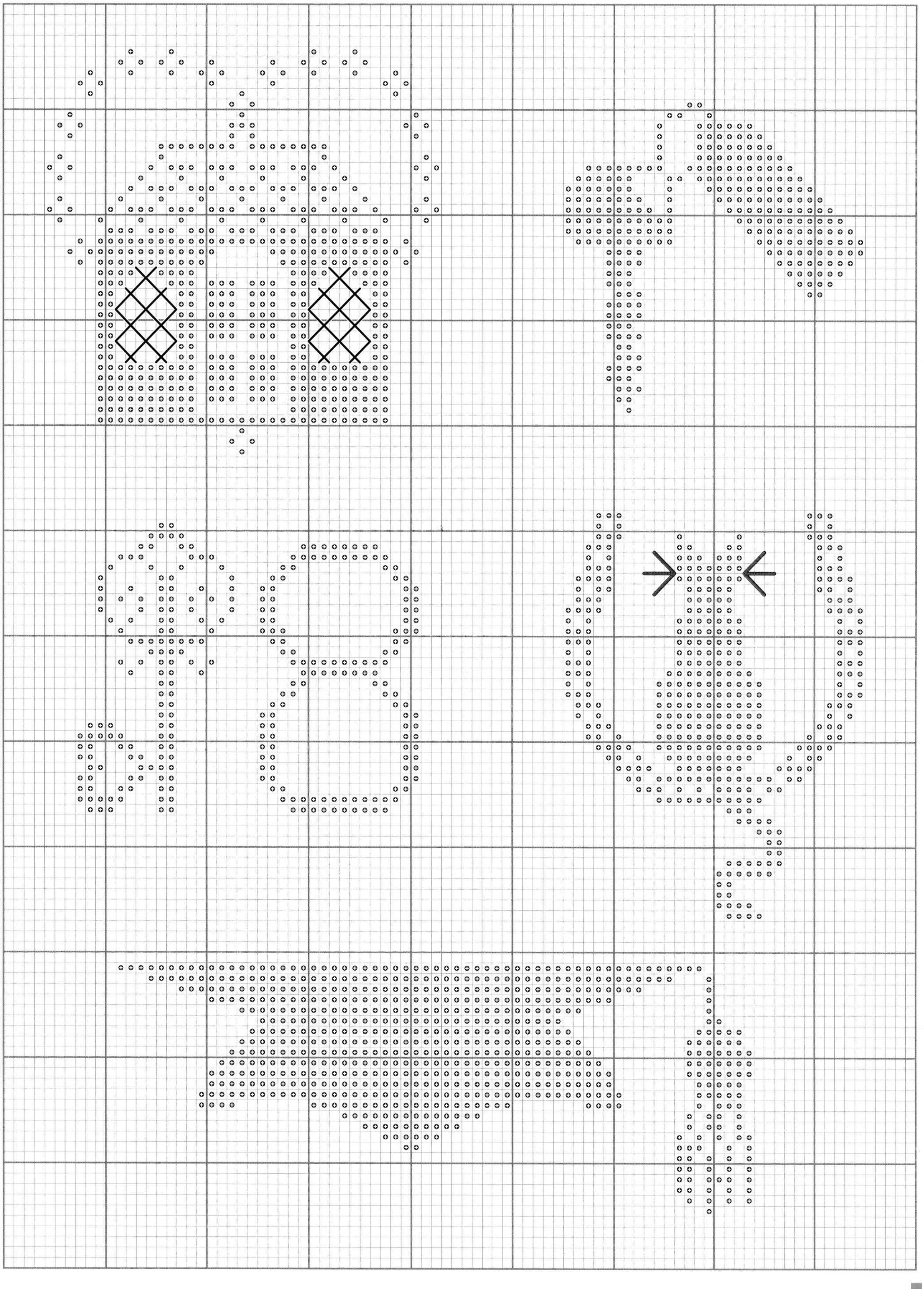

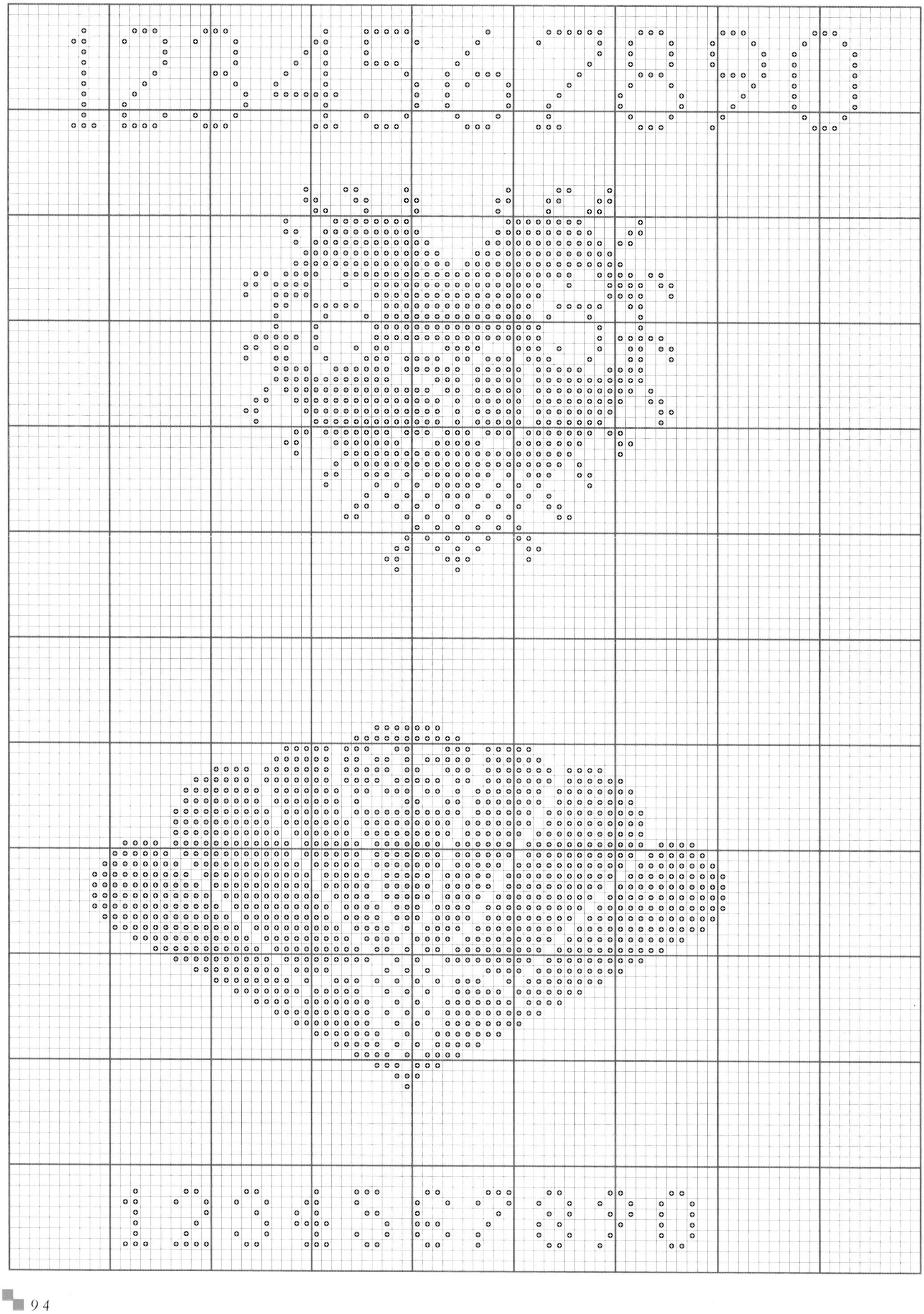

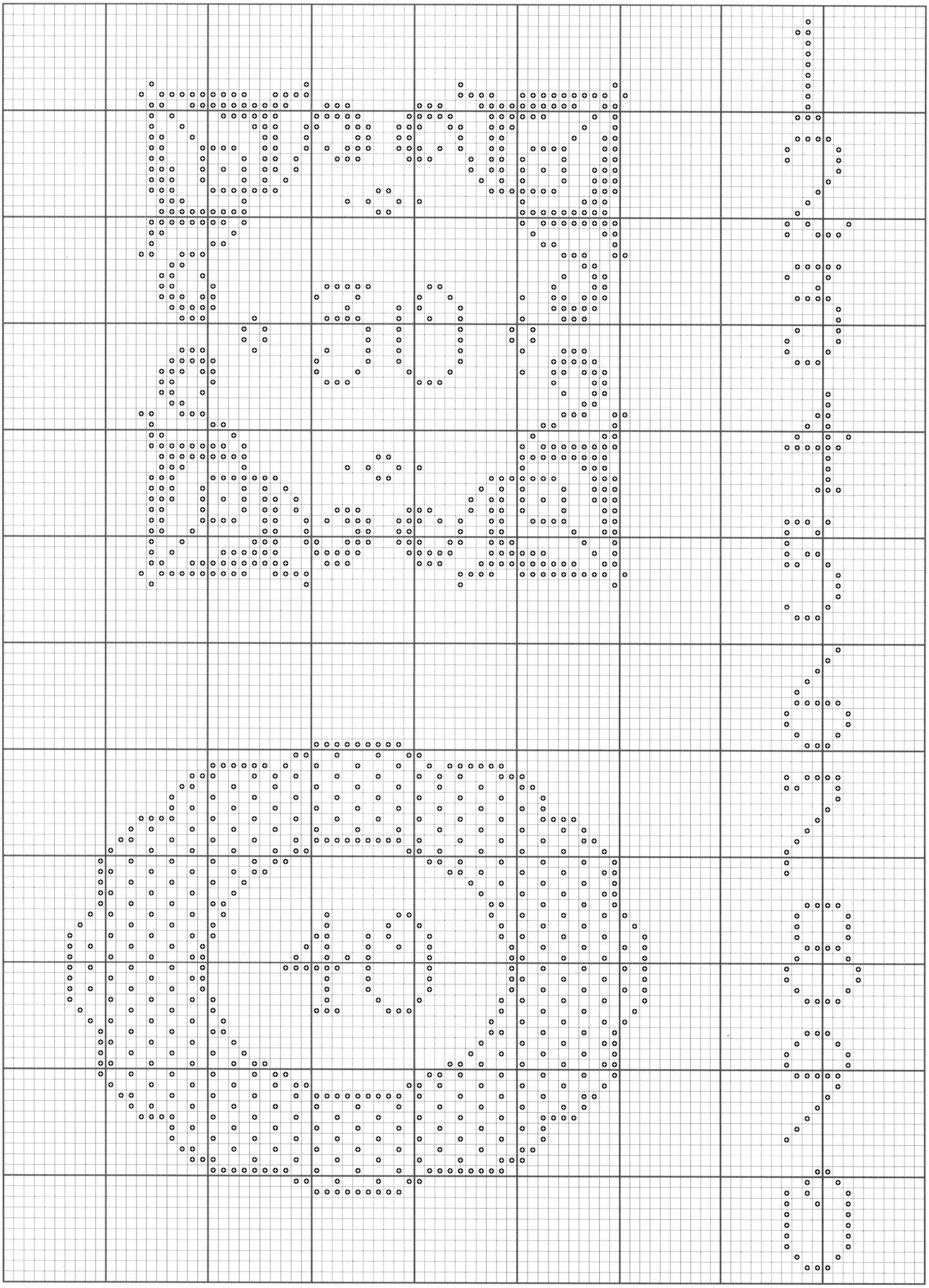

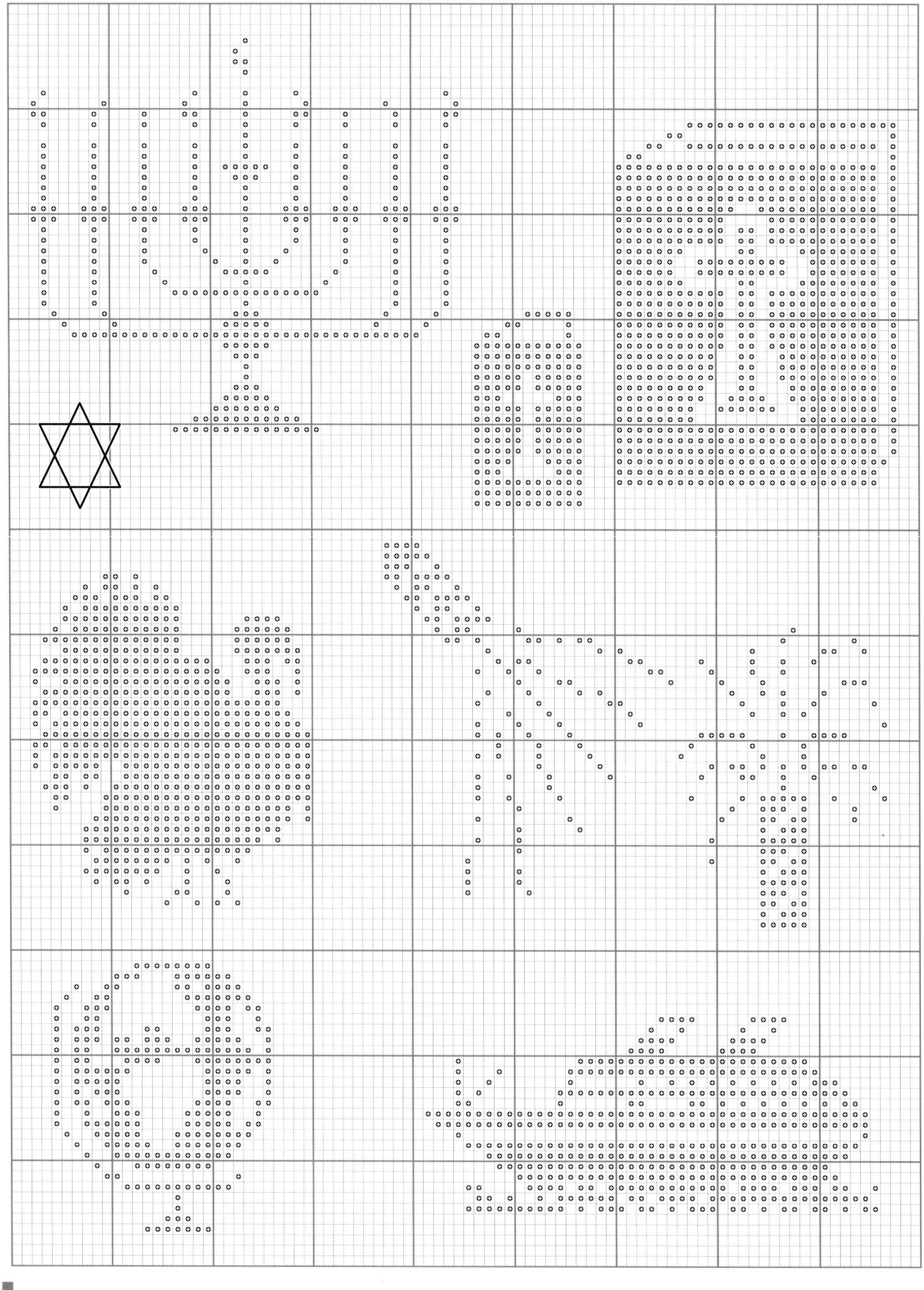

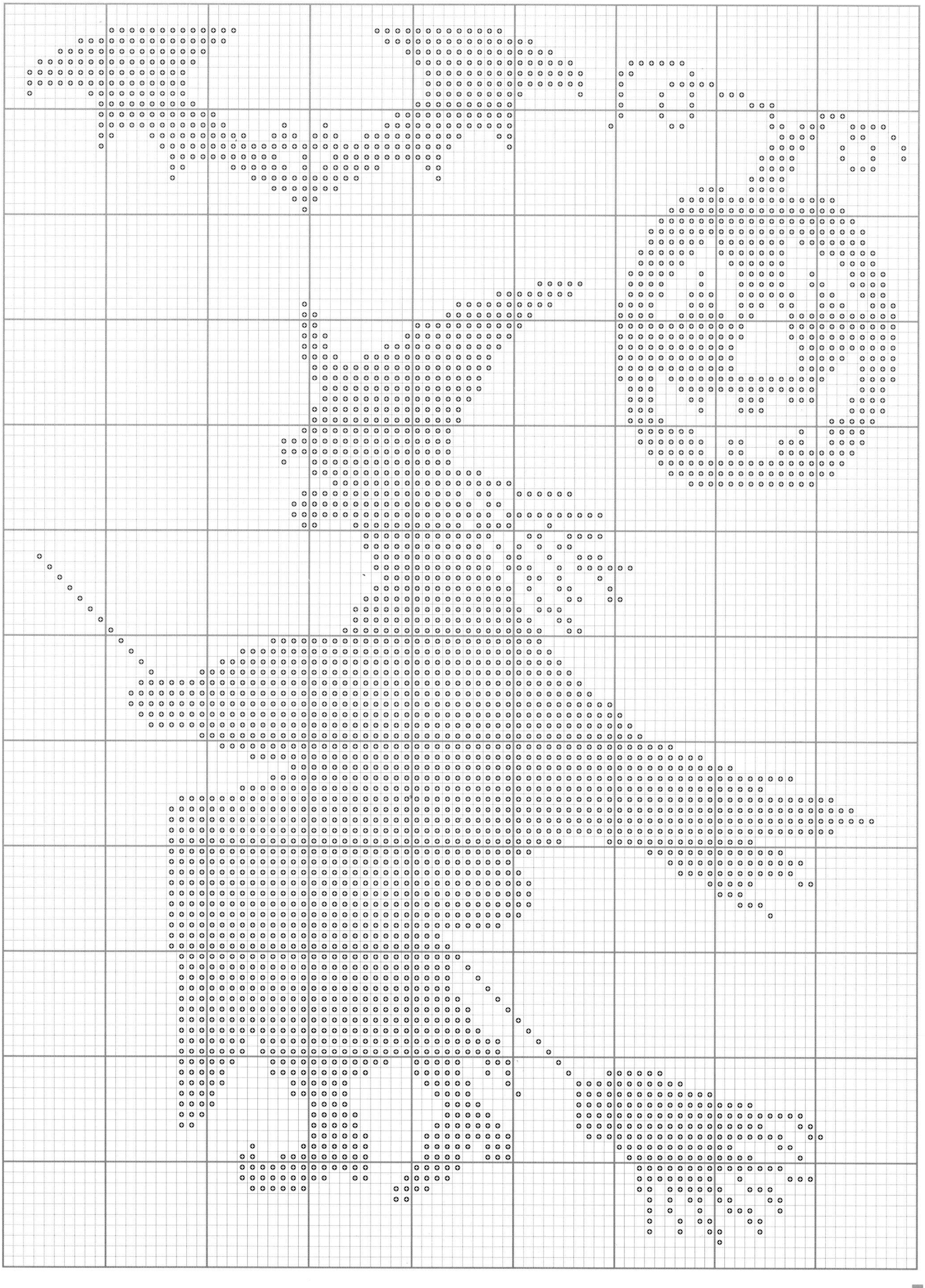

CHRISTMAS JOY

THIS SEASONAL CHAPTER contains all the baubles, trees, stars and festive motifs you'll ever need to create the perfect Christmas. Charts include a lovely range of nativity scenes, which are perfect for creating a traditional feel in the home at this special time of year. There are also some pretty snow-scene motifs with snowflakes galore – ideal for cards and tree decorations. When making up projects refer to Finishing and Making Up.

× × × × × ×   *Stitching notes*   × × × × × ×

Christmas dinner is the occasion for an impressive table setting. Dark navy Aida fabric has been used to make a table mat which has been stitched with twinkling snowflakes in two strands of Madeira Rainbow Glissen Gloss. The serviette holder has a candlestick motif stitched on the same Aida with one strand of metallic silver thread, while a name place card features parcel motifs in gold metallic thread. Christmas trees and sprigs of holly decorate a cake or candle band, stitched in one strand of green metallic thread on a green-edged 14 count Aida band (from Fabric Flair). Pretty, hanging decorations are quick to stitch and make great gifts for fairs and fêtes. A 22 count Hardanger fabric in Christmas red has been stitched with one strand of metallic gold thread and mounted into Christmas-shaped frames from Framecraft.

× ×

VARIATIONS ON A THEME

■ Any of the Christmas motifs could be made into cards or gift tags, or for a family celebrating their first Christmas with a new baby, you could stitch any of the designs onto a bib or booties. The festive designs can also be adapted for coasters or perhaps a key-ring as a quick stocking filler. Alternatively you could stitch several of the designs to make a festive sampler or Advent calendar using one of the borders from pages 112–121 to edge the designs. A nativity motif of a wise man following the Bethlehem star could be stitched for a special card or picture.

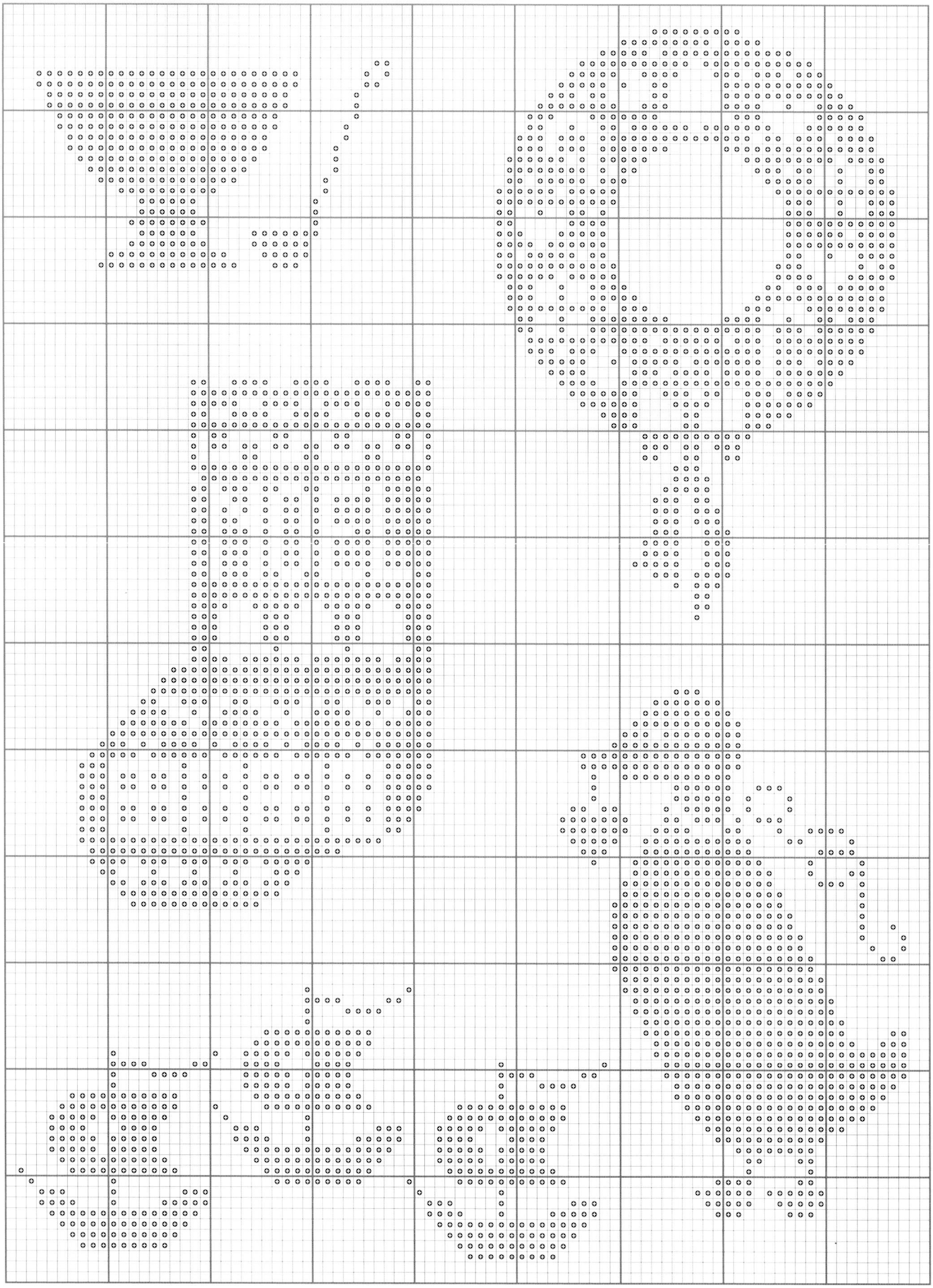

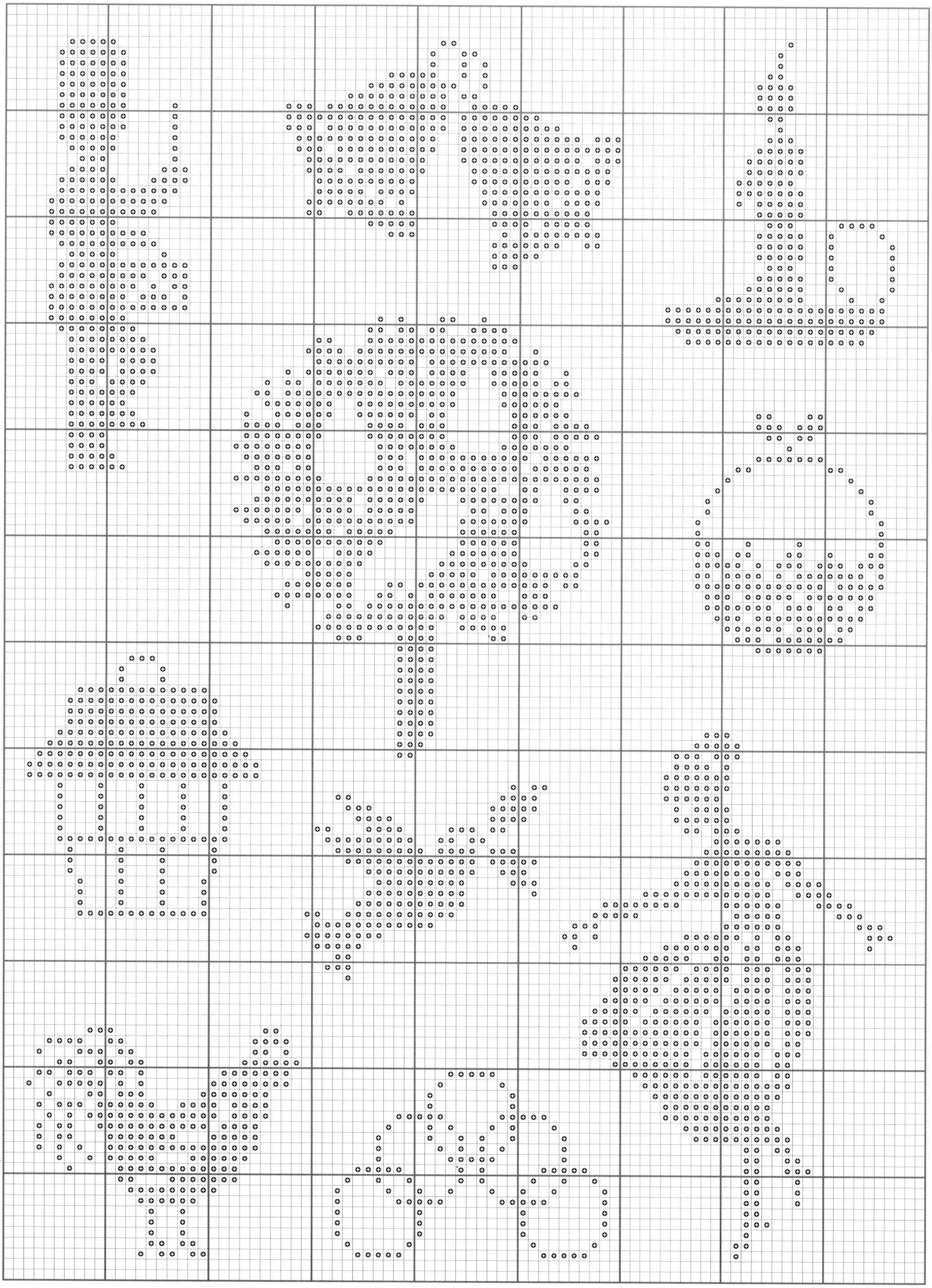

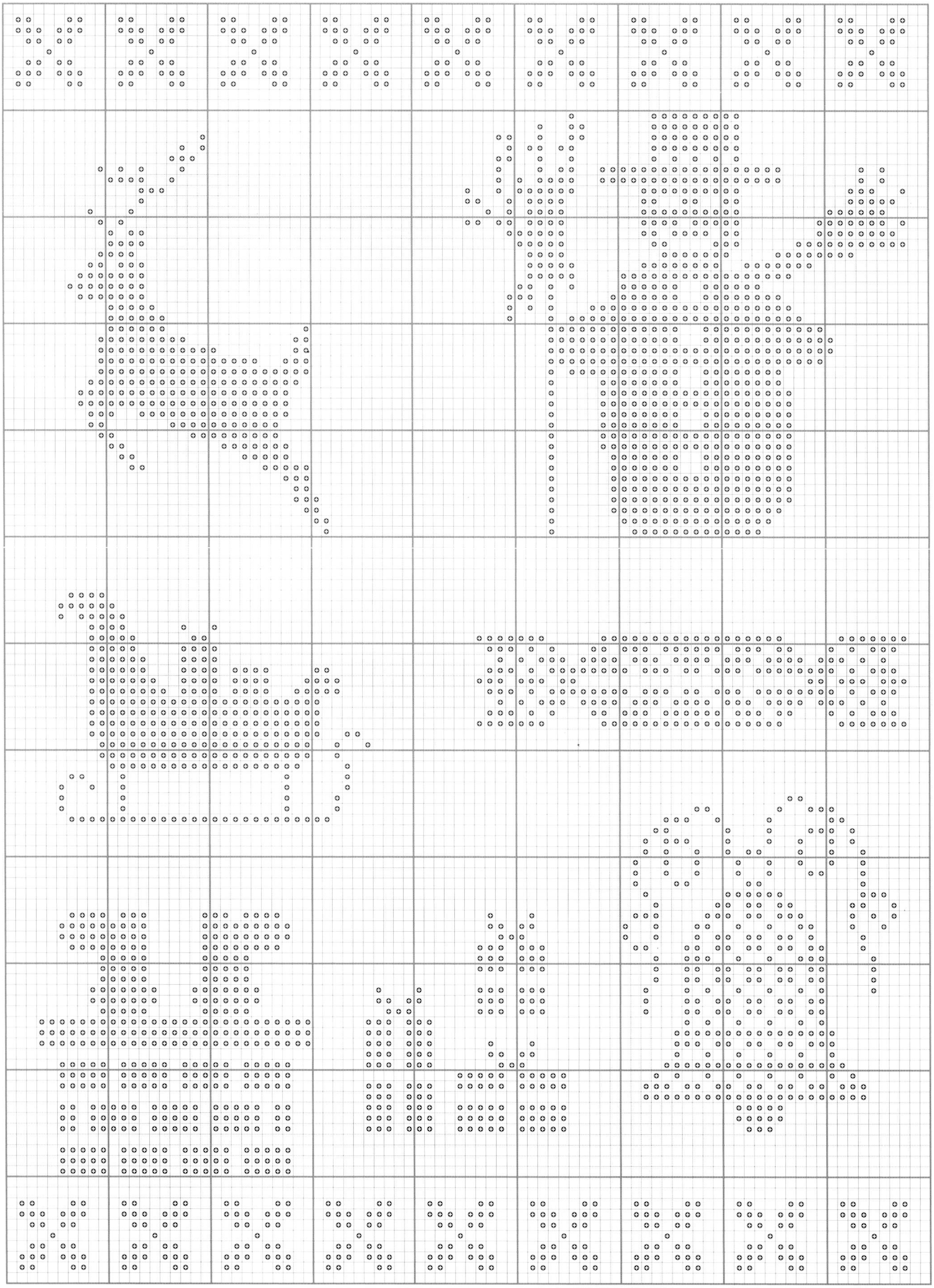

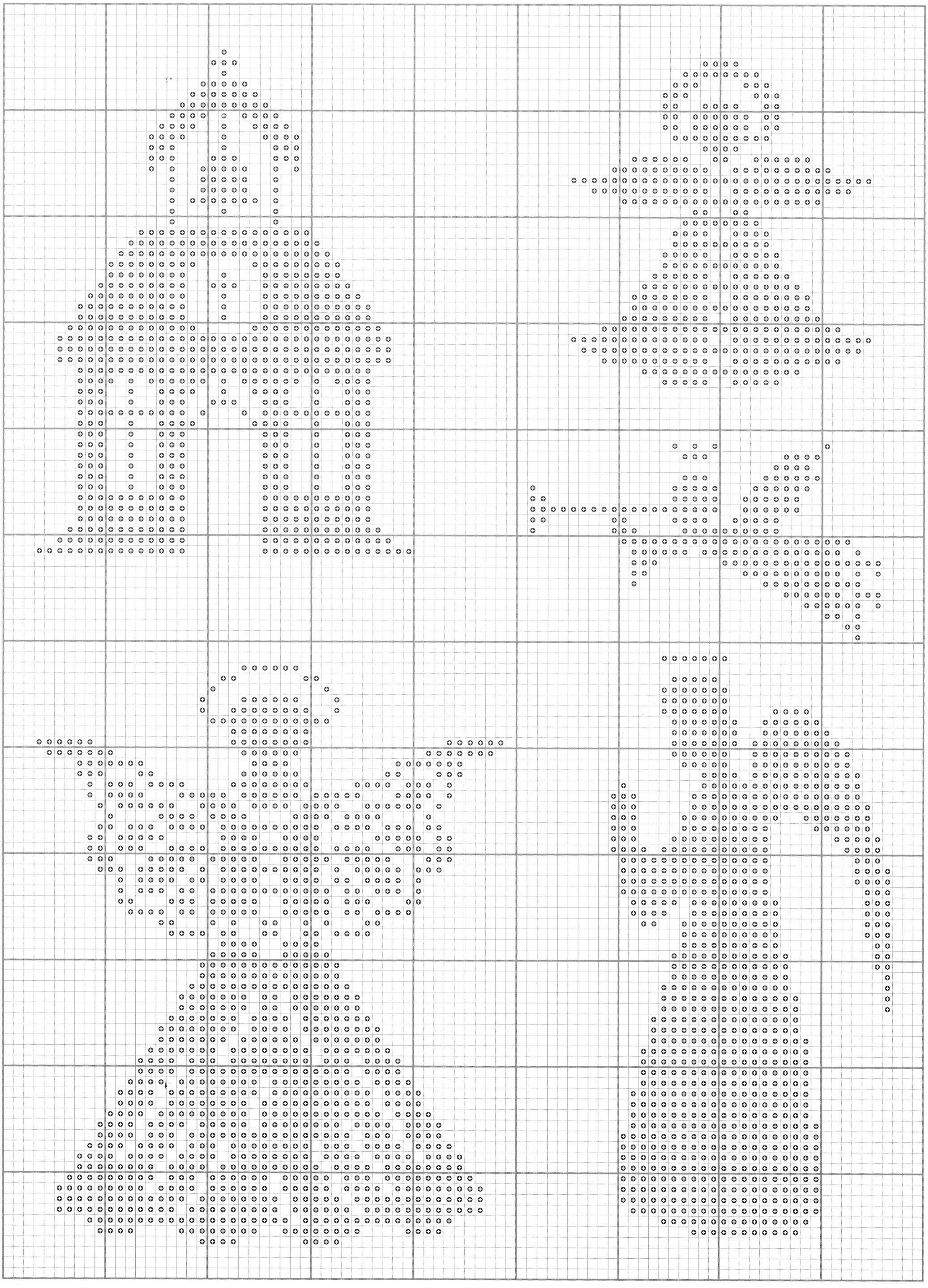

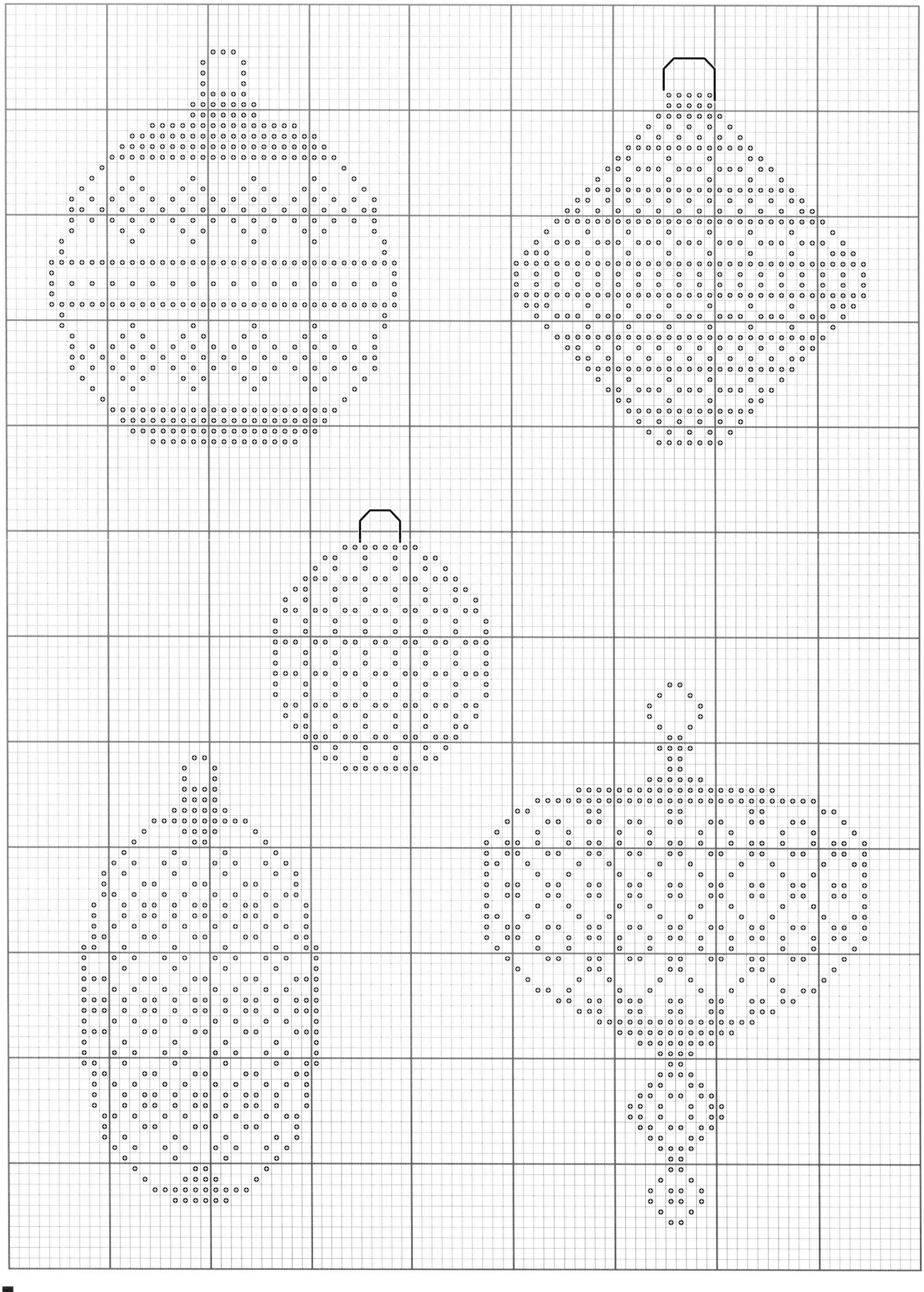

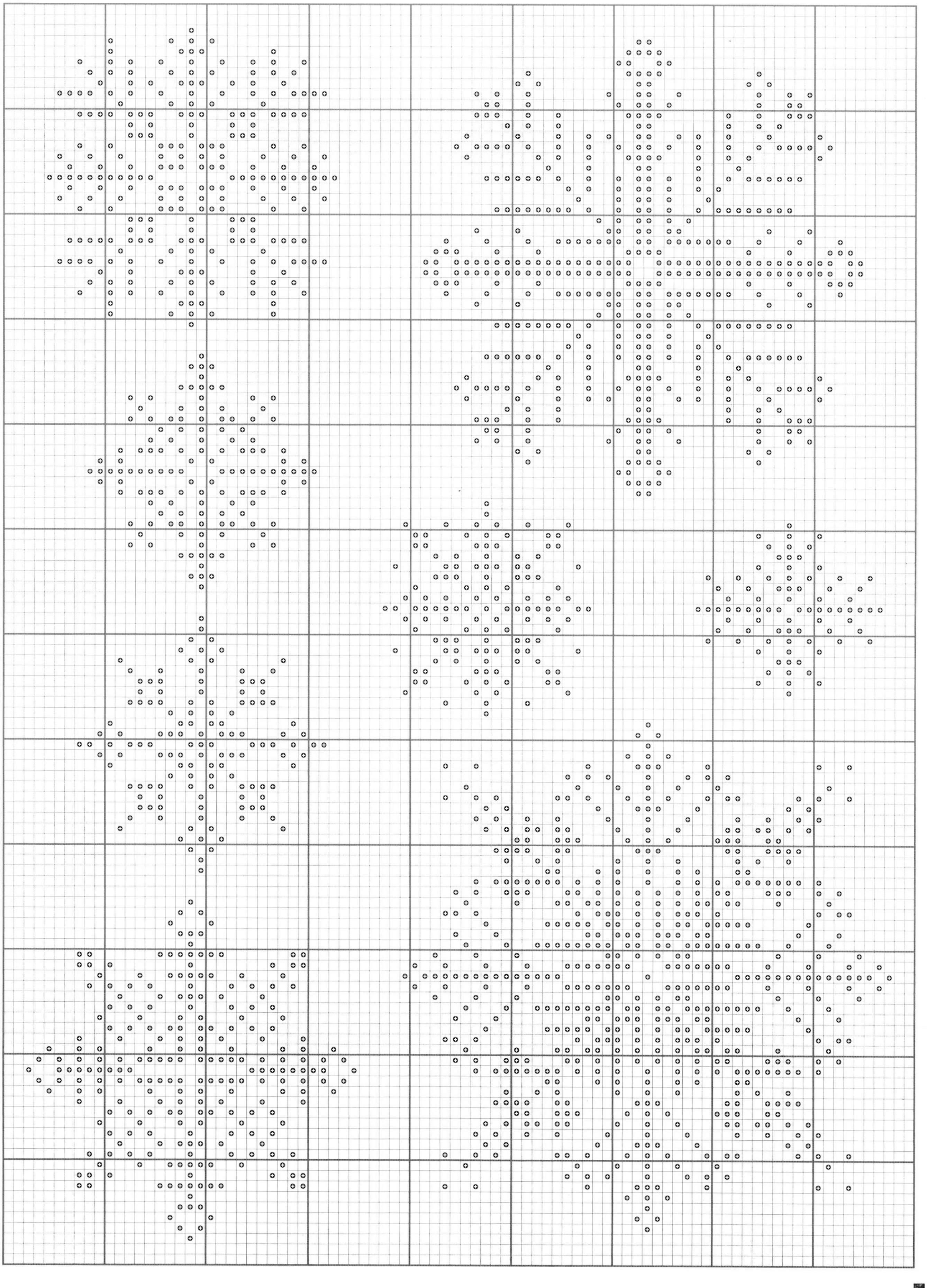

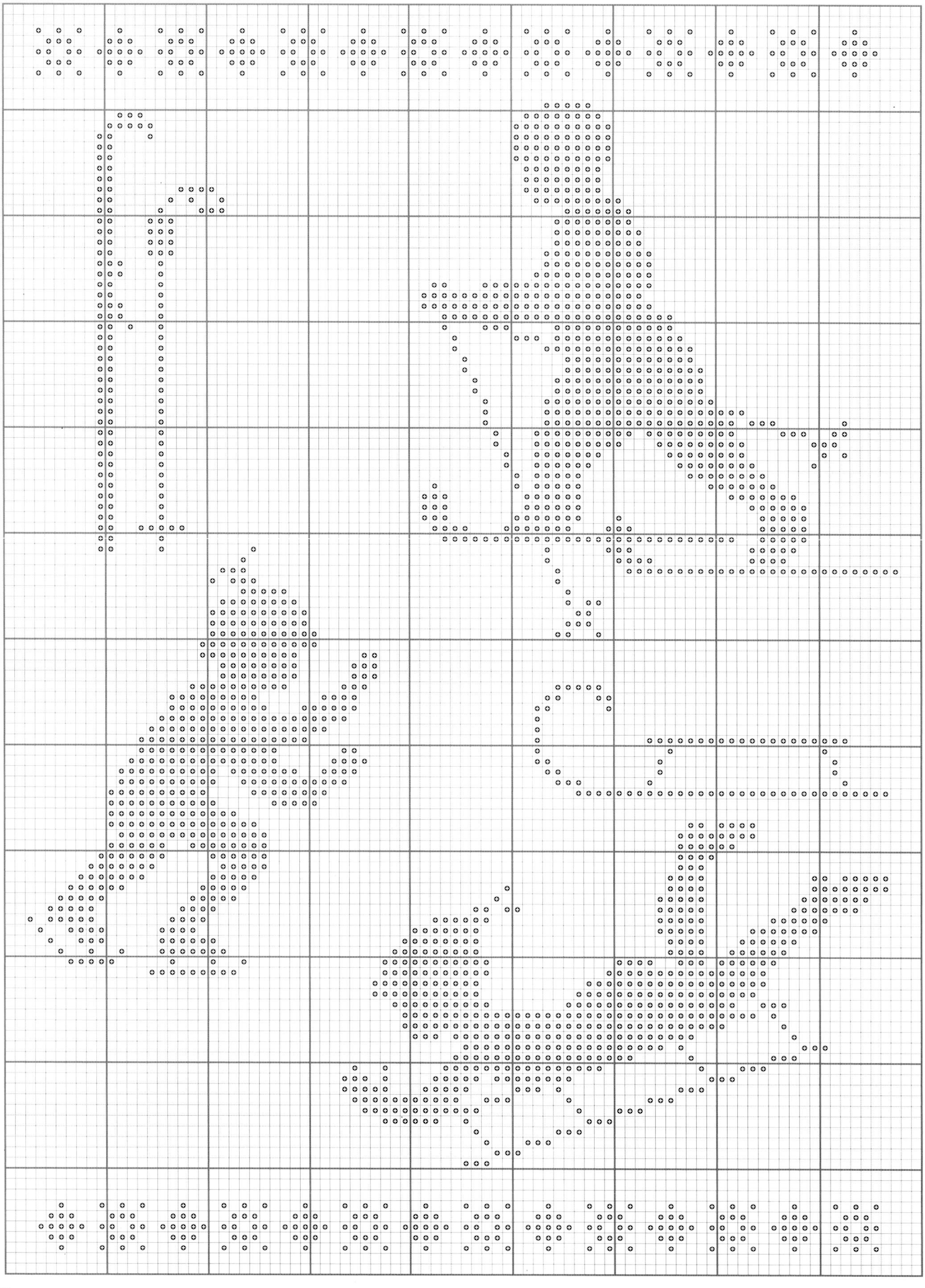

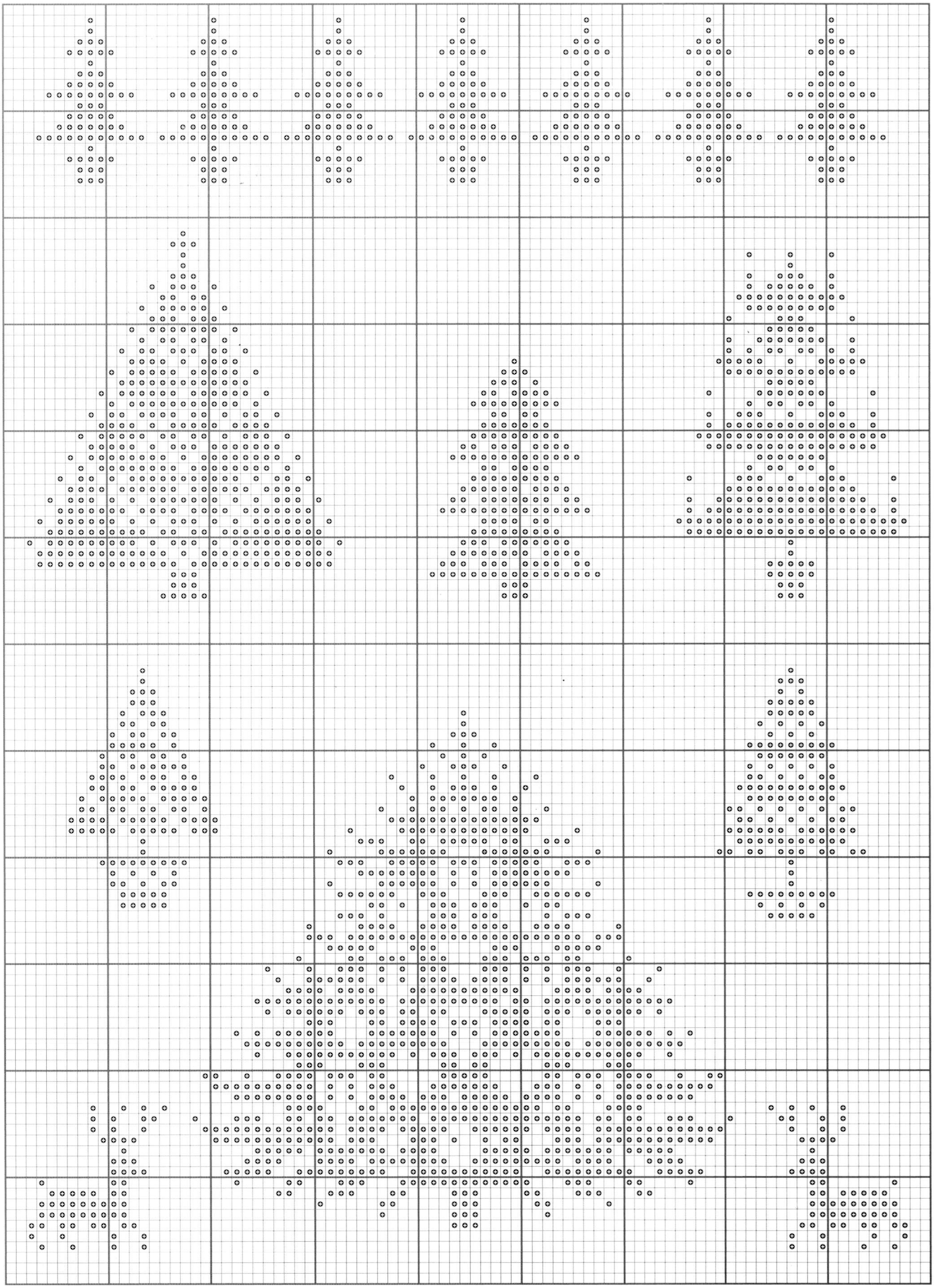

BORDERS GALORE

THIS CHAPTER contains a wonderful range of fun and decorative borders which have countless uses. The borders range from simple animal footprints and flowers to themed motifs, such as the sea and sampler-style images, and also more elaborate, geometric designs. A selection of useful alphabets has been included, ideal for personalising your work, creating samplers and making cards. When making up projects refer to Finishing and Making Up.

× × × × × × *Stitching notes* × × × × × ×

Ideal for carrying wine into the garden on a summer's day, a bottle holder has been decorated with a heraldic border stitched on 14 count Aida with one strand of plum Flower thread. A simple straw hat has been enlivened with a band of charming hedgehogs stitched on 28 count cream linen using two strands of chocolate brown stranded cotton. Continuing the nature theme, a border of flowers encircles a plant pot, stitched with one strand of natural coloured variegated thread over two threads of 32 count cream linen. Many of the border designs may be used as single motifs, as shown on the ivory coloured jar lacy from Framecraft which has been stitched with cherries using two strands of red stranded cotton.

× ×

VARIATIONS ON A THEME

■ Use the borders to bring colour and interest to household items, particularly towels, tea towels, bed linen and curtain tie-backs. Stitch a long border on a linen or Aida band and use it to decorate the edge of a shelf or dresser. Single motifs or small sections of the borders could be used to decorate items such as coasters and desk accessories. Alternatively multiple repeats of a border could be used to edge a piece of work or to frame a central motif. Try using the Native American motifs to create a photograph frame.

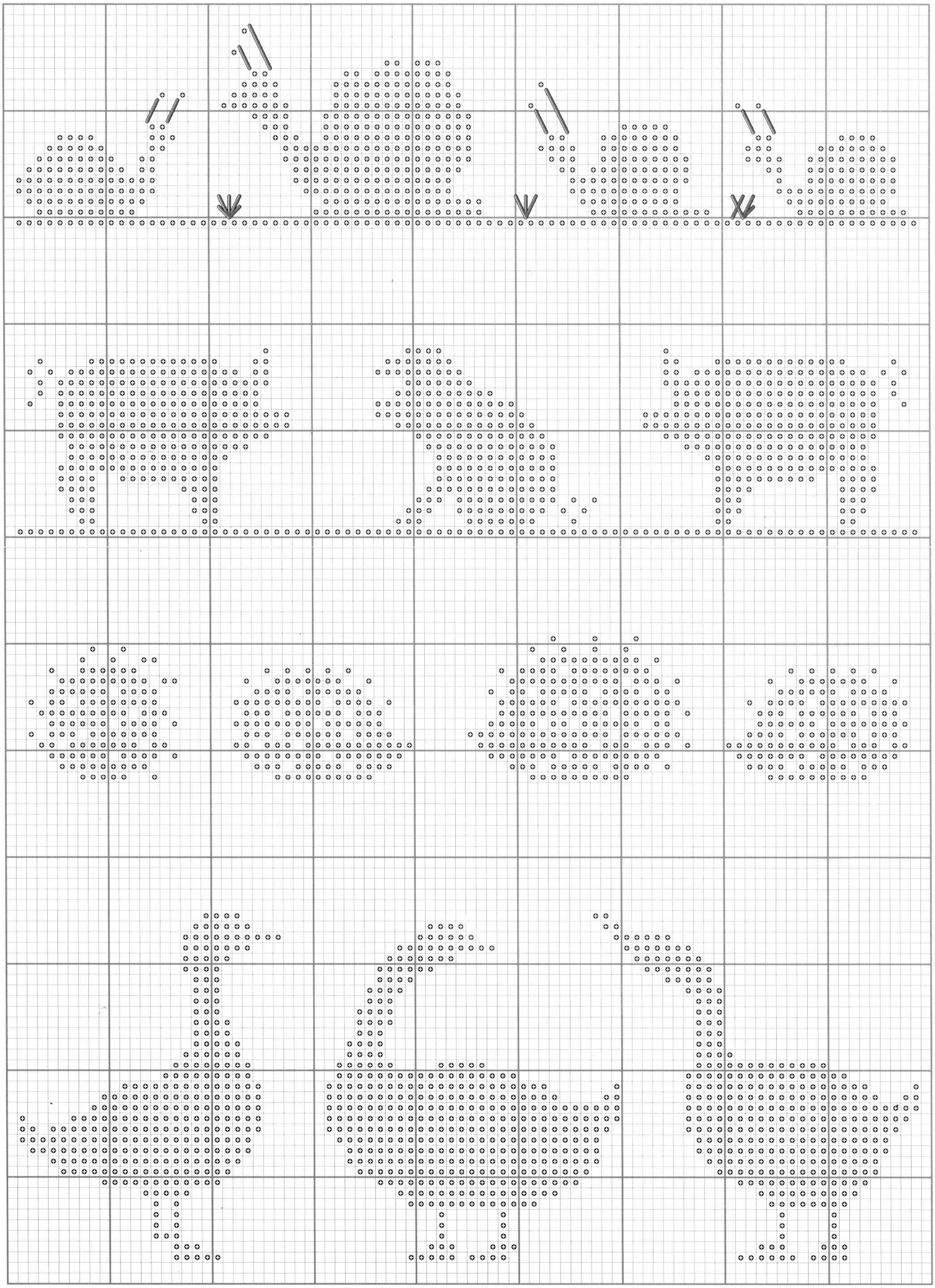

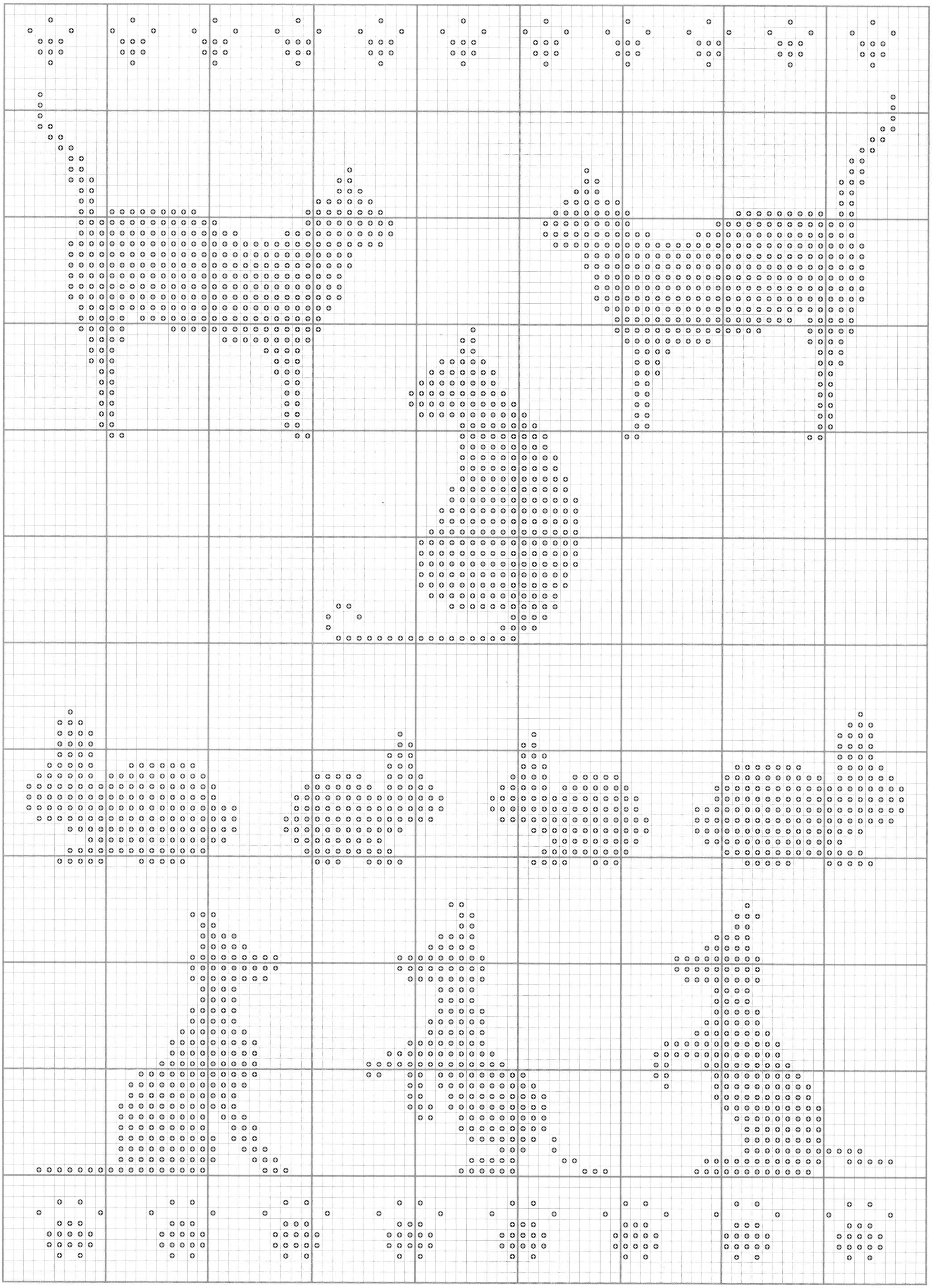

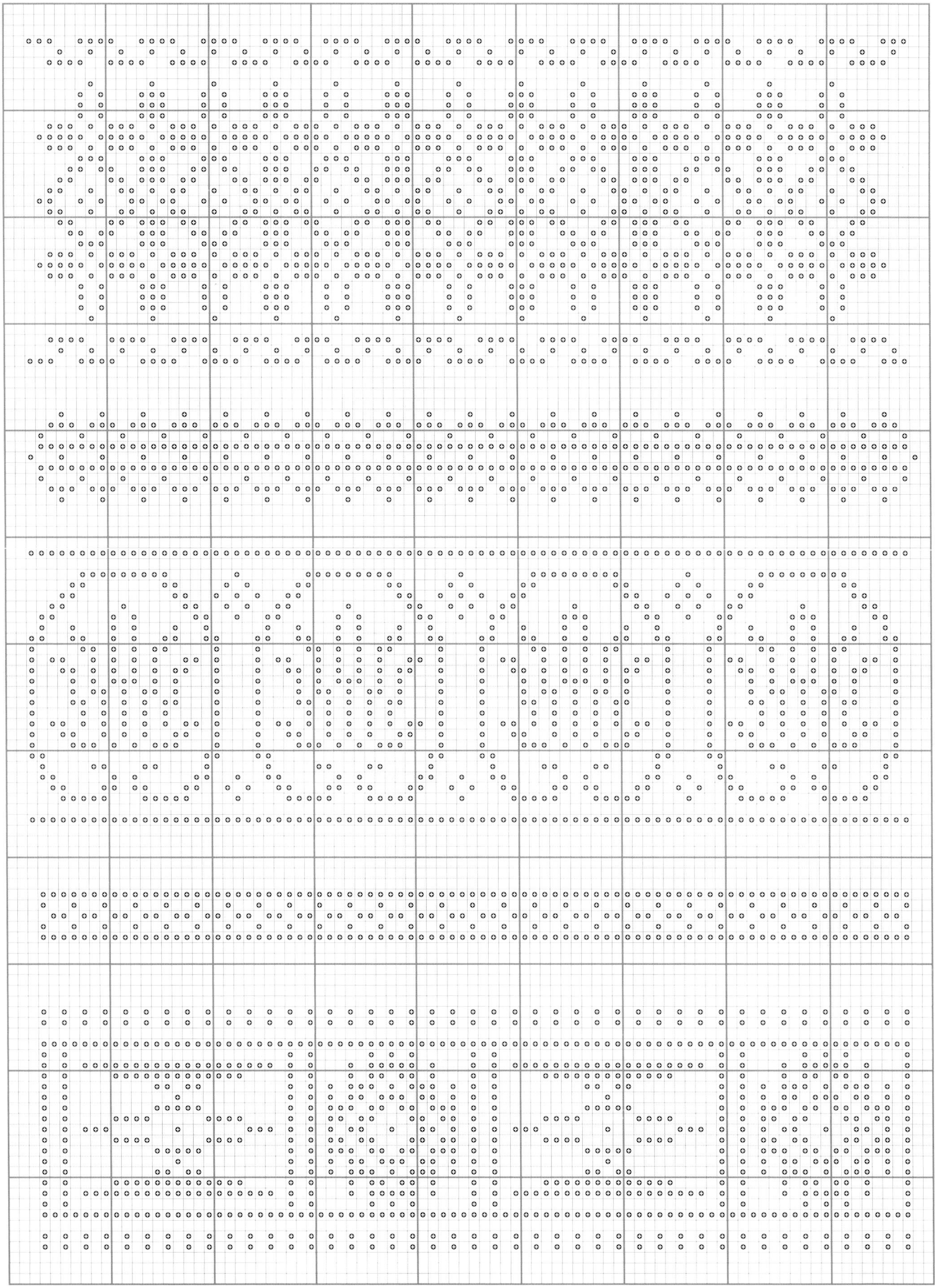

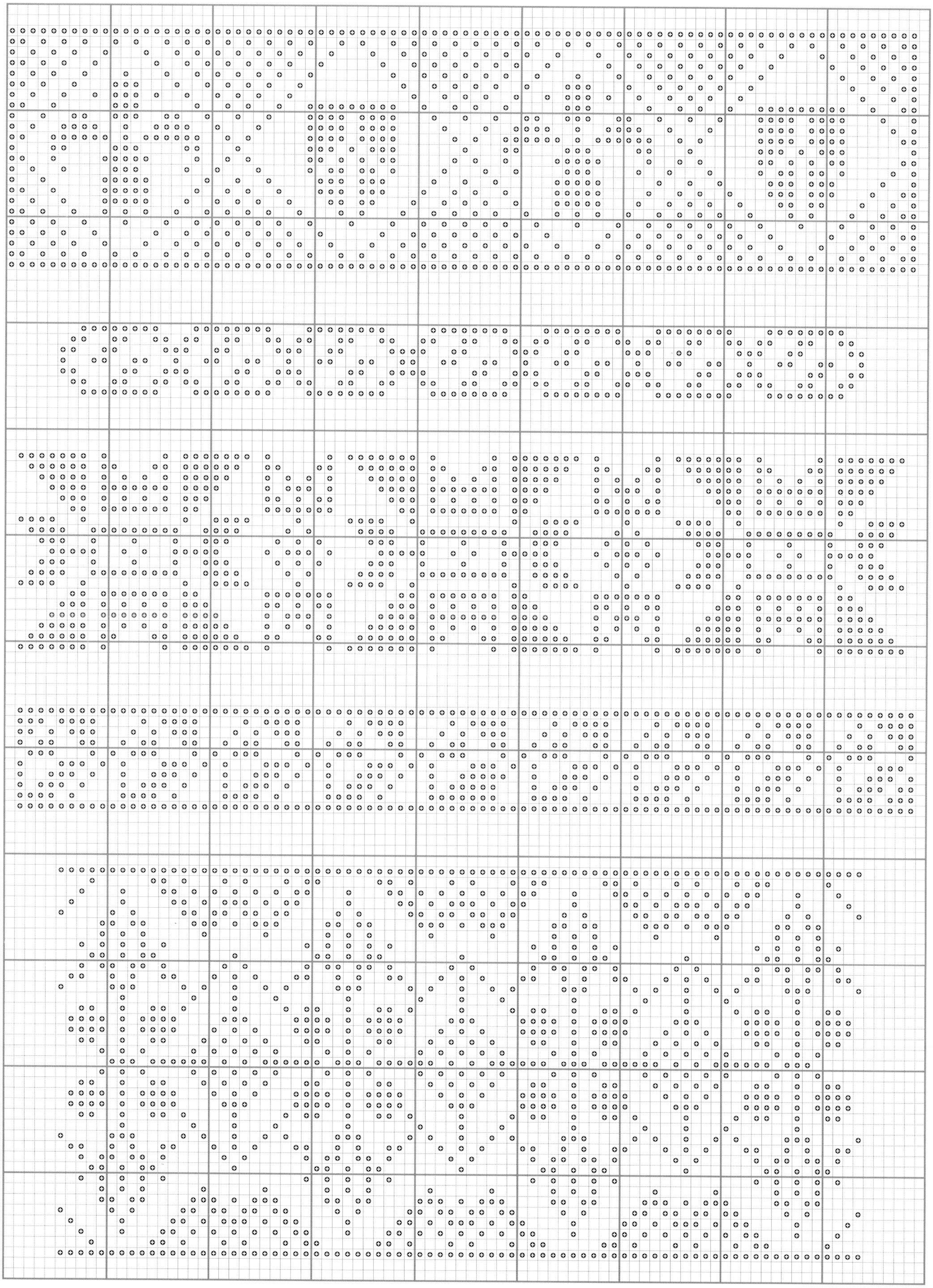

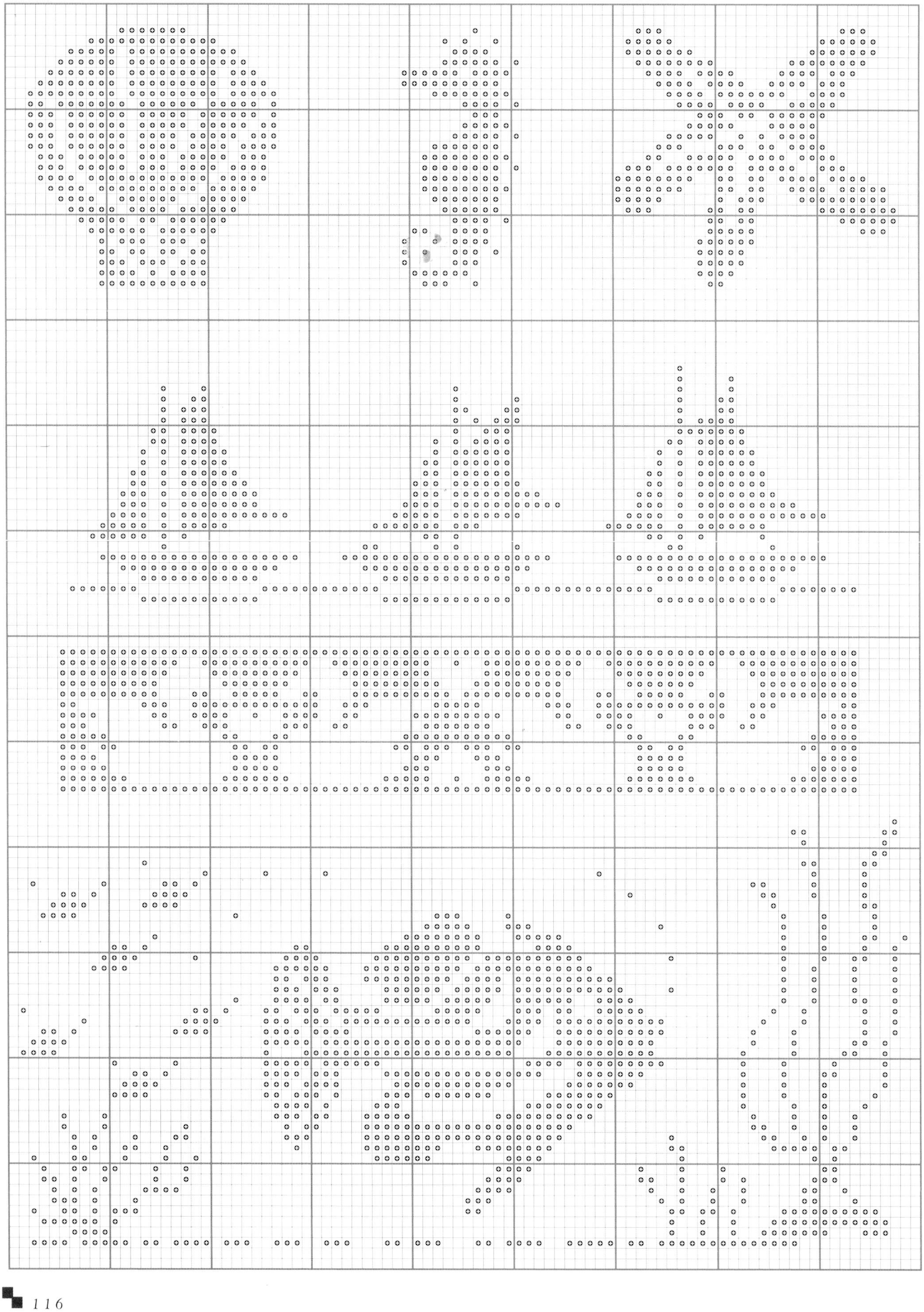

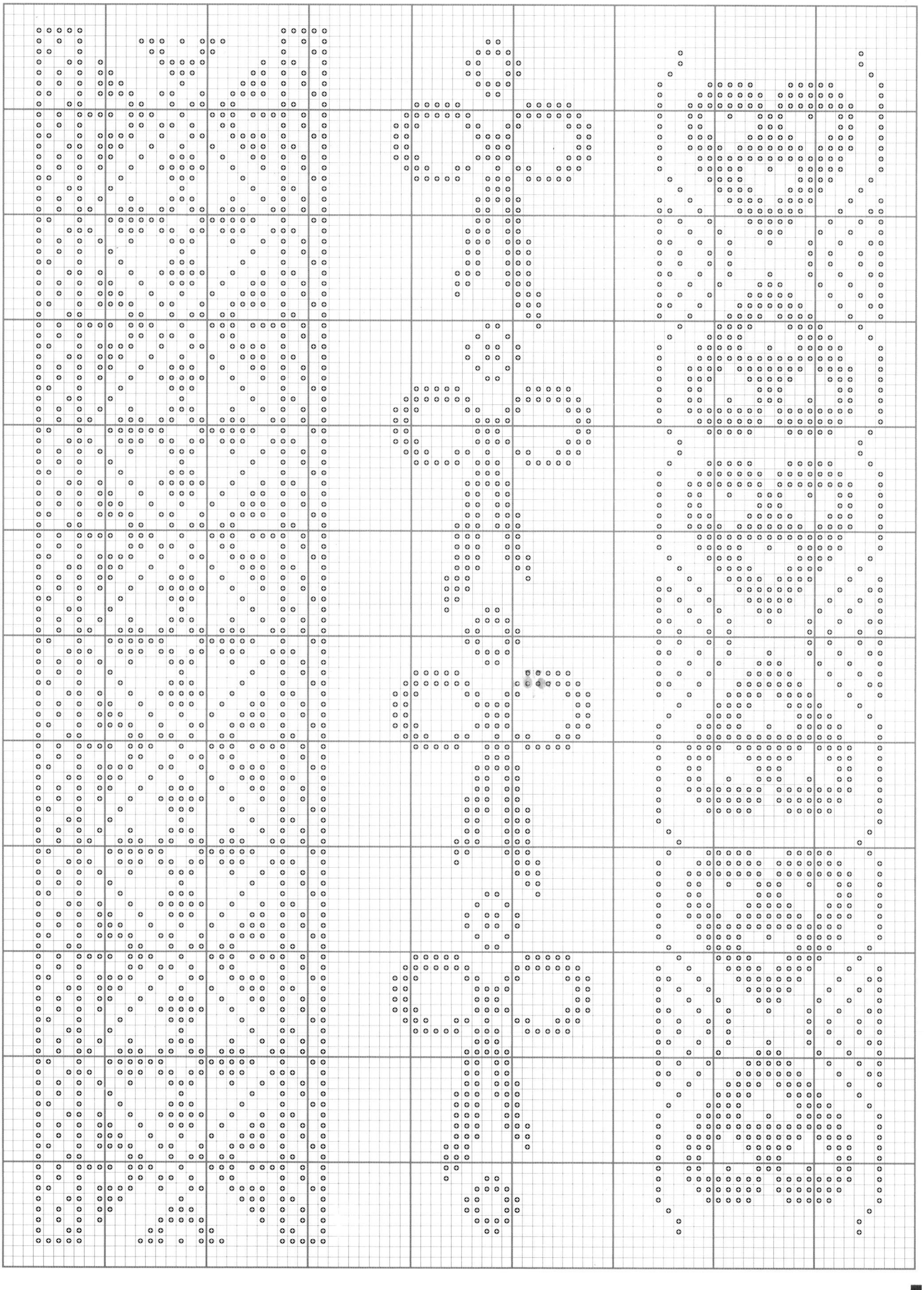

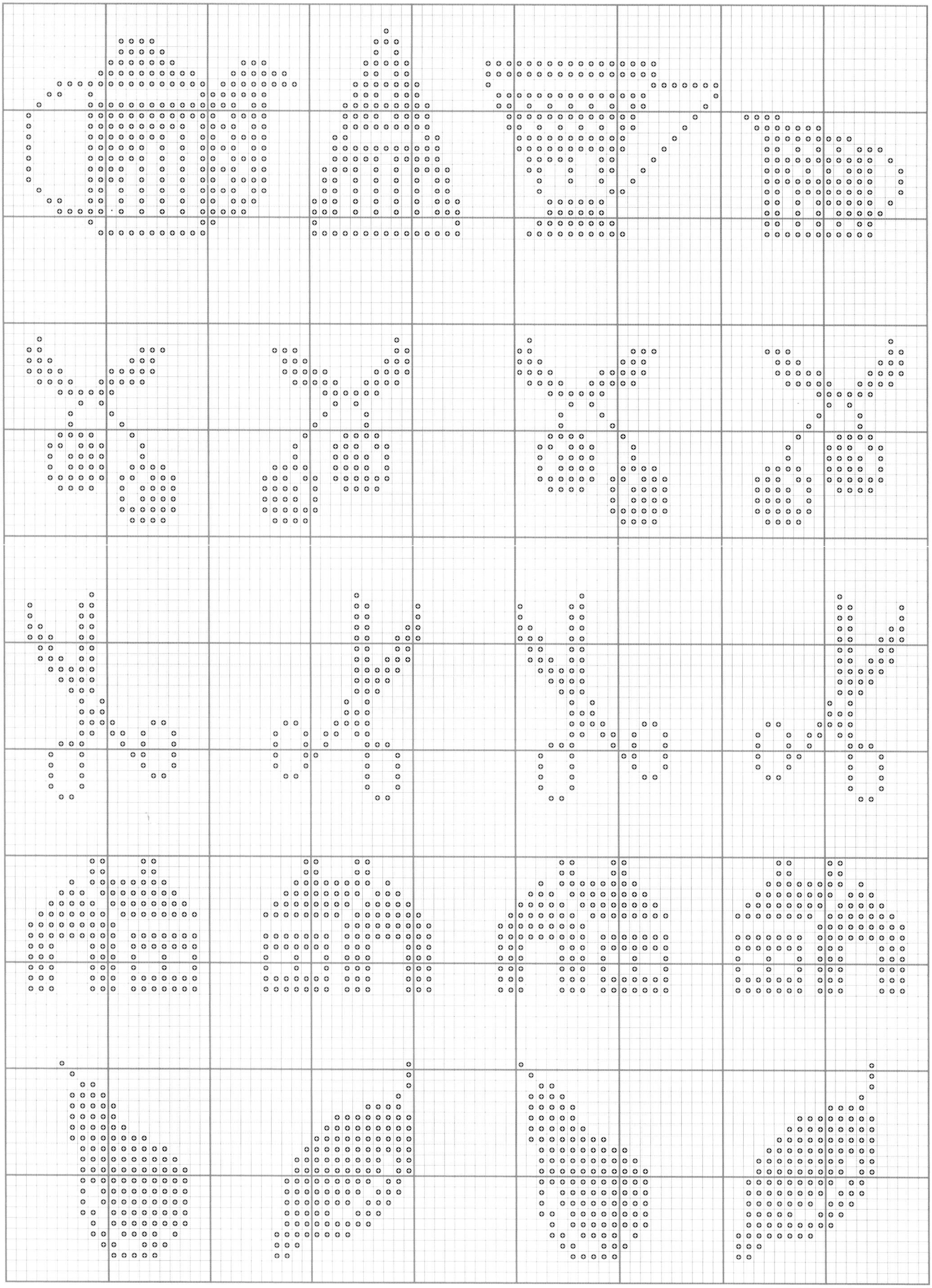

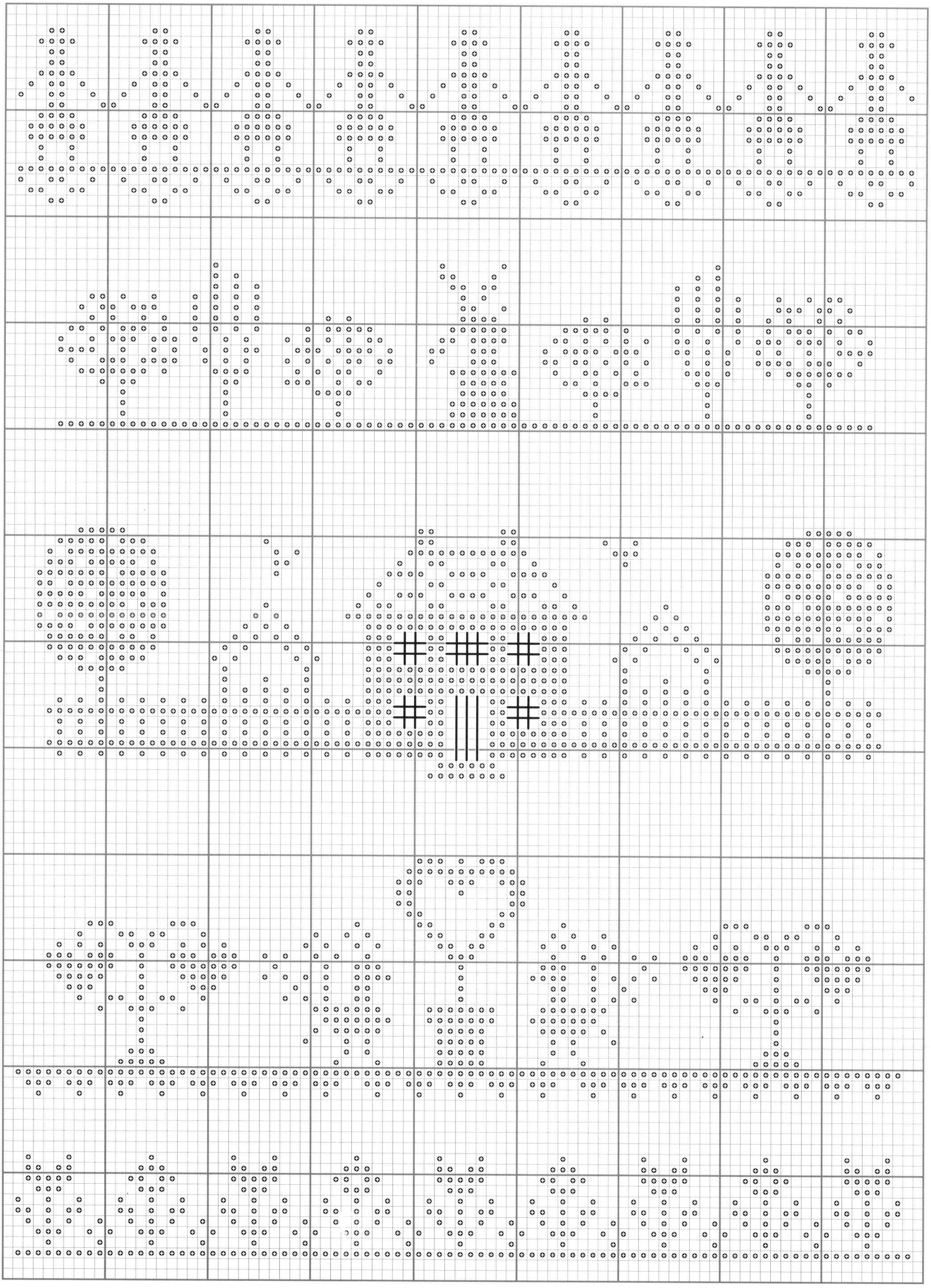

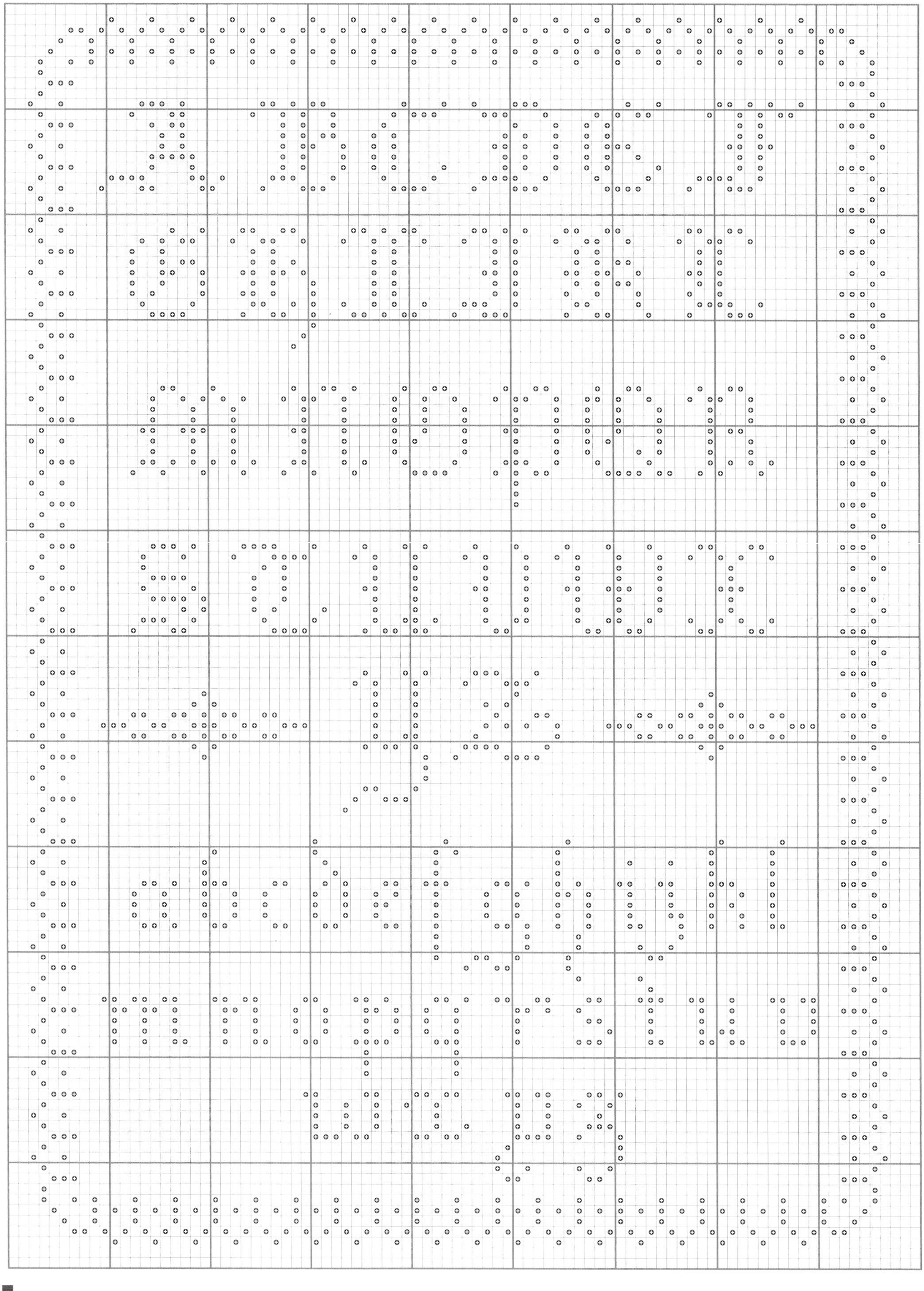

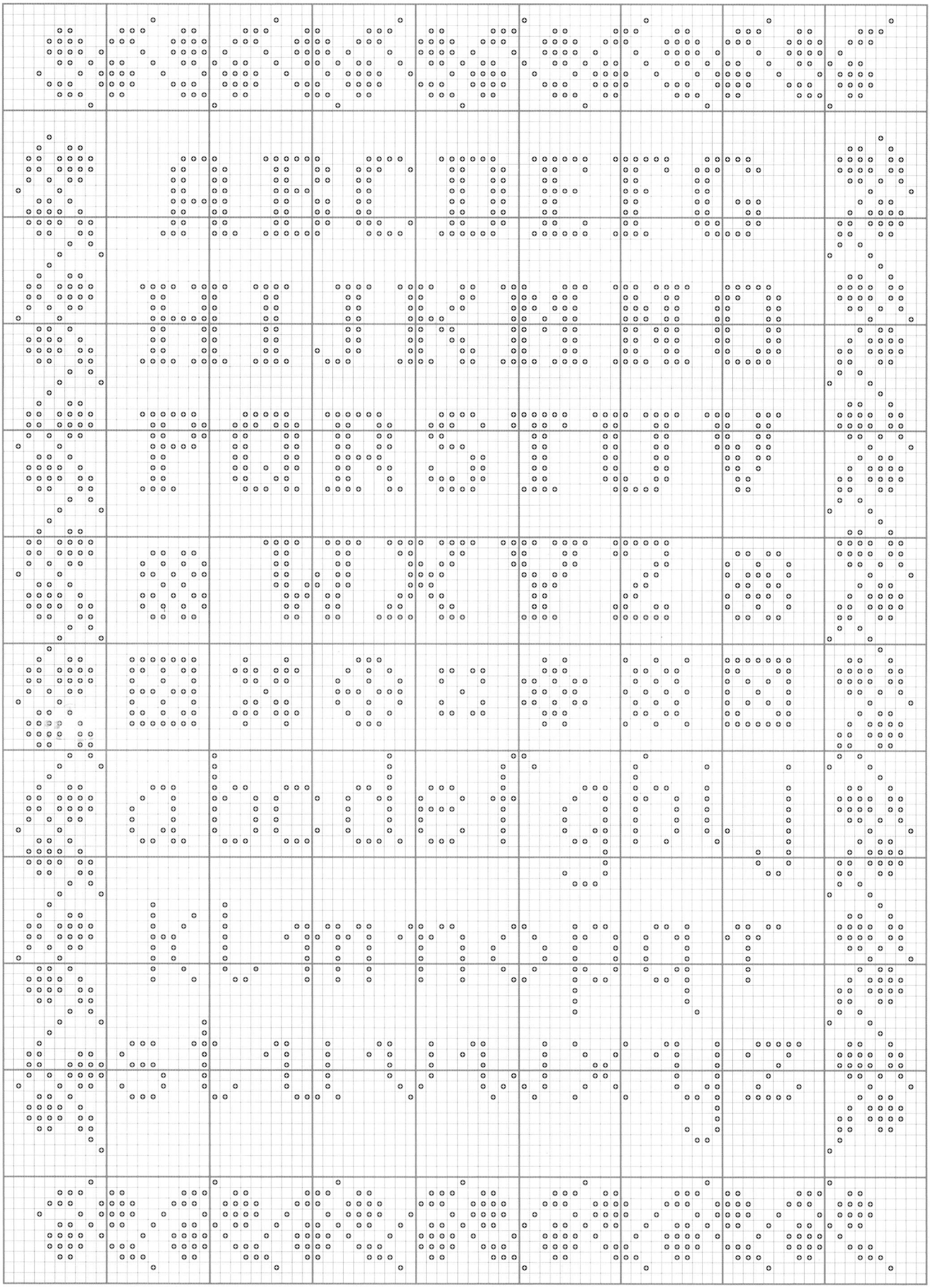

FINISHING & MAKING UP

A S YOU CAN SEE by the projects throughout this book, cross stitch silhouettes can be displayed in a wonderful variety of ways. Some are mounted in pictures, others are displayed in commercial products, of which there is a wide selection on the market today. Other designs are made up into items such as bags, book covers and cushions. This section gives general instructions for making these items. Specific quantities of materials needed cannot be given as this will depend on the size of your embroidery and the item you are making, and the stitching fabric will be of your choice – Aida or evenweave. You will need basic sewing equipment and threads.

CARING FOR EMBROIDERY

If your work is a little grubby after stitching freshen it up by washing in warm water using a mild detergent. Rinse thoroughly and then gently roll out excess moisture in a towel. Whilst still just damp iron the embroidery on the reverse side on a soft towel under a clean tea towel.

STRETCHING AND MOUNTING

Small projects will not require stretching and if they need to be mounted onto board prior to framing, can simply be attached using double-sided adhesive tape. Larger pieces of work will benefit by being taken to a professional picture framer. If you prefer to do it yourself you need to attach embroidery to a board before framing. Whichever method you choose, the work must be centred and stretched evenly.

FRAMING

There are some wonderful frames and mounts available today and the way a design is framed can greatly affect the end appearance. You may have stitched a design specifically to fit a frame you already have, or you may feel able to do the framing yourself, but in most cases it pays to take your work to a professional framer.

MAKING A SACK BAG

This style of bag, used for the Wizard Toy Sack on page 54, is simple to stitch and has many different uses. You could make the bag from Aida or evenweave fabric, embroidering your design directly onto the fabric, or make the bag from an ordinary fabric and sew on an embroidered panel, perhaps fraying the edges of the embroidery for a decorative effect. The instructions below are for a sewn-on piece of embroidery.

You will need
Sufficient fabric for the front and back of the bag
Length of cord or ribbon

1   Decide on the size of your bag and cut out two rectangles of fabric allowing 4cm (1½in) seam allowance all round. Stitch your piece of embroidery onto the front piece.
2   With right sides of the rectangular pieces together, pin and stitch the sides and bottom of the bag, matching the edges for a neat finish. Press the side seams open.
3   Fold the top edge over to the wrong side by 6mm (¼in). Press, then fold over again to form the top of the bag. Pin in place and sew two rows of parallel stitching around the top to form a casing. Turn to the right side. Snip the side seam between the lines of parallel stitching, binding the cut edges with buttonhole stitches or over-stitching.
4   Thread a length of cord or ribbon through the channel and secure the ends with a knot.

MAKING A TUBE BAG

This bag is basically a lined tube with a circular base. The outer bag is made from main fabric and the inner one from lining fabric. The Fuchsia Bag on page 12 was made this way. The instructions below are for a bag made from an ordinary fabric with a sewn-on piece of embroidery.

You will need
Sufficient fabric for the tube and circular base
Sufficient lining fabric for the tube and circular base
Length of ribbon or cord

1   Cut a rectangle of fabric and sew your embroidered piece centrally on it. With right side facing inwards fold the rectangle in half and stitch a 3cm (1¼in) seam along the short edge to create a tube. Trim and press the seam open. Repeat with the lining fabric.
2   Cut a circle from fabric slightly larger than the base of the tube and with right sides together, pin the circular base to the tube sides, machine stitch together and trim off excess fabric. Repeat for the lining. You now have two bags.
3   Turn the fabric tube right side out and place the lining

tube, wrong side facing outwards, inside the main fabric tube. Turn the top edges in to meet each other, to form a seam with the lining fabric fractionally below the top of the fabric tube. Slipstitch the edges together.

4   Cut a narrow band from main fabric the same length as the circumference of the bag. Press under a 6mm ($\frac{1}{4}$in) hem all the way around the fabric strip. Machine the strip onto the outside of the bag using two parallel lines of stitching to form a channel near the top of the bag. Turn the strip over to the inside of the bag and stitch in place (see fig 1). To finish, thread a length of ribbon or cord through the channel and tie with a knot.

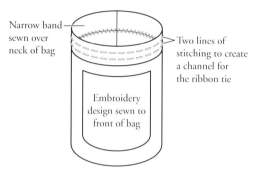

Narrow band sewn over neck of bag

Two lines of stitching to create a channel for the ribbon tie

Embroidery design sewn to front of bag

Fig 1   Making the neck of the tube bag

MAKING AN ENVELOPE BAG

This simple type of bag has been made for the nightdress case on page **55** and the seed packet holder on page **41**. The embroidery is worked directly onto the fabric of the bag.

> ### You will need
> *Long rectangle of stitching fabric*
> *Lining fabric the same size as stitching fabric*
> *Velcro and buttons (optional)*

1   Cut a long rectangle of stitching fabric allowing a 4cm ($\frac{1}{2}$in) seam allowance. Stitch your cross stitch design at one end of the fabric, 5cm (2in) from the short edge. When the embroidery is complete, trim the fabric 2.5cm (1in) from the cross stitch on three sides.

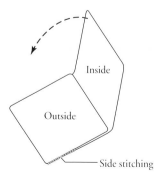

Inside

Outside

Side stitching

Fig 2   Sewing up an envelope bag

2   Cut a piece of lining fabric the same size as the stitched fabric. With right sides facing, pin the cross-stitched fabric and lining fabric together. Tack and then machine stitch 1.25cm ($\frac{1}{2}$in) from the edge, leaving a gap for turning. Trim the seam to 6mm ($\frac{1}{4}$in) for less bulk and cut across the corners. Turn through to the right side and ease out the corners with a blunt tool, then press lightly on a towel. Slipstitch the gap closed.

3   Fold the lower third of the panel up and neatly oversew the lower side seams with small hemstitches or overstitches (see fig 2). The top third of the bag simply folds over, though you could make a fastening by sewing on small pieces of Velcro or buttons.

MAKING A BOOK COVER

A book cover is a great way of displaying cross stitch silhouette designs. You could make the whole book cover from Aida or evenweave fabric, embroidering your design directly onto the fabric, or make the cover from ordinary fabric and sew on an embroidered panel. The instructions given below are for a sewn-on piece of embroidery.

> ### You will need
> *Paper for template*
> *Sufficient fabric to cover your book*
> *PVA glue (optional)*

1   Measure the book to be covered by placing it fully opened onto a piece of paper and drawing around it, adding 4cm ($1\frac{1}{2}$in) extra. Cut out the shape.

2   Using the paper as a pattern, cut a piece of fabric and turn down and stitch a 1.5cm ($\frac{1}{2}$in) hem all round.

3   Place the fabric temporarily in position around the book and mark where your embroidered piece needs to go. Sew on the embroidered piece.

4   Slipstitch the cover flaps to form pockets for the front and back jackets of the book (see fig 3). For a permanent result you could use PVA glue to stick the fabric directly onto the book.

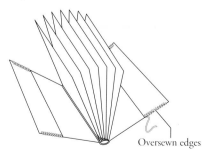

Oversewn edges

Fig 3   Sewing the book cover

MAKING A TRINKET ROLL

A trinket roll (see page 71), is useful for keeping all sorts of precious items safe. The roll is made from stitching fabric, with the embroidery worked before making up, and is a finished, opened-out size of approximately 31 x 25cm (12 x 10in).

You will need
Stitching and lining fabric – see sizes below.
Four lengths of ribbon for ties
Velcro for fasteners

1   Cut the following pieces of fabric, adding an extra 2cm (³/₄in) to all pieces for seam allowances (see also fig 4):
Piece of stitching fabric 31 x 25cm (12 x 10in) for the roll.
Piece of lining fabric 31 x 25cm (12 x 10in) for the roll.
Piece of stitching fabric 12.5 x 25.5cm (5 x 10in) for the large bottom pocket.
Piece of stitching fabric 7.5 x 25.5cm (3 x 10in) for the smaller top pocket.
Piece of stitching fabric 5 x 25.5cm (2 x 10in) for top pocket flap.

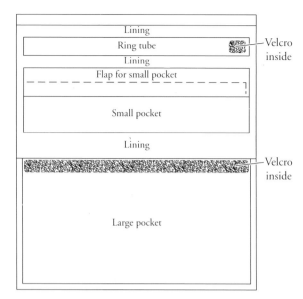

Fig 4   *The parts making up the inside of the roll*

Piece of stitching fabric 5 x 25.5cm (2 x 10in) for the ring tube.
2   Embroider your design or designs onto your stitching fabric for the front of the roll and the inner pockets.
3   Turn under a 2cm (³/₄in) hem along the long edges of the pockets and flap.
4   Fold the fabric for the ring tube in half lengthways, pin and stitch together, then turn through to the right side.
5   Place the pockets on the lining, wrong side up with the hemmed edge at the top, and sew along the bottom. Bring the pockets up and pin the ends before tacking in position.
6   Place the top pocket flap onto the lining, wrong side up with the hemmed edge at the top. Position the flap so that when it is turned down the top of the small pocket is covered. Turn the flap down and pin before tacking into position.
7   Sew a small piece of Velcro to one end of the ring tube and a corresponding piece on to the lining. Pin and tack the tube into position at the opposite end to the Velcro, ensuring that slipstitching is hidden.
8   Pin the lining onto the wrong side of the embroidered fabric. Machine stitch around the edge, leaving a gap for turning out. Check you have caught the edges of the pockets on both sides (but only on the side away from the Velcro for the ring tube).
9   Trim across the corners and any excess fabric around the sides, then turn to the right side and slipstitch the opening.
10   Attach ribbon ties to the ends of the roll 2.5cm (1in) in from the sides of the roll. Roll up the trinket roll and tie with the ribbons.

The Taj Mahal design featured
on the front of the trinket roll
(the chart is on page 80)

MAKING A MOBILE

Many of the designs in the book are perfect for creating a mobile, as the Teddy Mobile on page 54 shows. Basically the mobile is made from embroidered shapes sewn back to back with card and wadding in between.

You will need
Thin card
Stitching fabric
Wadding
Metal hoop 25cm (10in) approx.
Length of ribbon or braid
Decorative trimming, e.g. bobbles (optional)

1 Choose a shape and a size for the mobile pieces, such as a circle, square or diamond, and cut a template from thin card (suitably sized to house the design you've chosen). Using the template, cut twice as many card shapes as the number of shapes you are going to hang.

2 Using the card template, cut the same number of pieces of wadding as card shapes but trim them to be slightly smaller than the card shapes.

3 Cut the same number of pieces of stitching fabric but cut them 2.5cm (1in) larger than the card shapes. Cross stitch your designs onto the stitching fabric.

4 Run tacking stitches around the edge of all the stitched fabric pieces, about 1.5cm ($^1/_2$in) in, leaving long ends of sewing thread for pulling up. Take a card shape, put a wadding shape on top, then an embroidered shape right side up on top of that. Pull up the tacking thread so the embroidered fabric pulls tight around the card and wadding pieces, and tie off with a knot. Repeat this with the remaining pieces. (Thus, if you planned six hanging shapes in total for the mobile, you will have twelve padded shapes at this stage.)

5 Cut ribbon to a variety of lengths – long enough for hanging the shapes from the hoop and the hoop from the ceiling.

6 Attach a length of ribbon to the top of a padded shape and a trimming (such as a bobble) to the bottom, if using one. Then with right sides facing outwards, hand stitch two padded shapes together. Repeat this pairing for all the padded shapes.

Dedicated stitchers would not be without a pincushion by their side. By adapting the patchwork quilt motifs from the Favourite Pastimes chapter into a square, the centre is left empty, ready for pins and needles. Keeping with tradition, two strands of deep red stranded cotton has been used over two threads of a cream 28 count linen

7 Cover the hoop with ribbon or braiding. Position the embroidered shapes equally around the hoop and pin into position allowing them to hang at varying heights. You should have enough length of ribbons above the hoop to tie off at the centre, adding a loop for hanging from the ceiling. Check that the mobile is hanging horizontally and then stitch the ribbons in place around the hoop.

MAKING A CUSHION

Making a cushion is a lovely way to display embroidery. You could make the cushion from Aida or evenweave fabric, embroidering directly onto the fabric, or make it from ordinary fabric and sew on an embroidered piece. The travel pillow on page 70 was made in the following way.

You will need
Sufficient stitching fabric for the cushion front
Sufficient backing fabric for the cushion back
Lining fabric (optional)
Cushion pad
Trimmings (optional)

1 Stitch your cross stitch design onto a piece of stitching fabric the size required for the front of the cushion, adding 4cm ($1^1/_2$in) for a seam allowance.

2 Cut a piece of backing fabric for the back of the cushion to the same size as the front. With right sides facing, pin the front and back together. If using a lining, cut a piece of lining fabric to fit and pin this in position now. Machine or hand stitch around the edges leaving a gap along one of the sides for turning through to the right side.

3 Trim the seams to **1.5cm** ($^1/_2$in) and cut across the corners. Turn through to the right side and ease out the corners using a blunt tool. Insert a cushion pad and turn raw edges under and slipstitch to close.

4 To trim the cushion with lace or frills, position the trimming around the edges of the cushion when pinning the front and back together prior to sewing up. If using a braid, slipstitch it around the edges of the cushion once turned right side out, covering all the side seams.

MAKING A BAND

Stitching a border on a band is a perfect way of embellishing all sorts of objects, such as candles, cakes and flower pots, as you can see in the Borders Galore chapter. You can either use a ready-prepared band, available in various widths and with different coloured edgings, or cut a length of stitching fabric and hem the edges.

First, measure the length or circumference of the object you wish to decorate with the band. Next, stitch the required length of border from the centre of the band outwards. Once the embroidery is complete, stitch side seams to neaten the ends of the band. If using a length of stitching fabric, machine stitch seams along the lengths of the band. Sew on pieces of Velcro for fastening the ends. Alternatively fold the edges under along the length of your stitching and stick to the item with double-sided adhesive tape.

MAKING A BOOKMARK

Stitch your cross stitch silhouette design onto a suitably sized piece of fabric, then trim the fabric to within 1cm ($^1/_2$in) of the stitching all round. Hem all sides except the bottom. To make a shaped point at the bottom, turn under the bottom edge about 6mm ($^1/_4$in) and tack (ensuring that none of the embroidery is included). Find the seam centre point and bring the two corners together so they meet at the back. Slipstitch these two edges together. A tassel at the point makes a lovely addition (see right).

MOUNTING STITCHING INTO COMMERCIAL PRODUCTS

There are many, many different items available today which have been designed to display embroidery (see Suppliers page **127** for some addresses). Some of those used in this book include a money box, tray, hat, hair brush, mirror, trinket pot, glasses case, jar lacy, booties and bags.

To mount work in these products, you generally only need to follow the manufacturer's instructions, but it helps to back the embroidered work using iron-on interfacing as this strengthens the stitches and prevents fraying. Use a piece of interfacing roughly the same size as your stitched fabric, iron it onto the reverse side of the stitching and trim the fabric to size before mounting.

MOUNTING STITCHING IN A CARD

Mounting embroidery into a commercially made card is one of the simplest ways to display work. When the stitching is complete, press the work from the wrong side. Open out the card and check the design fits the opening. Apply a thin coat of glue or double-sided adhesive tape to the inside of the opening (see fig **5**). Put the embroidery into place, checking the stitching is central, then press down firmly. Fold the spare flap inside and stick in place either with double-sided tape or glue. Leave to dry before closing. Add any ribbons or trimmings as desired.

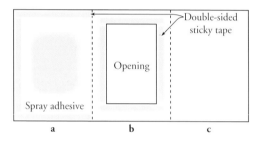

Fig 5 Mounting embroidery in a card

MAKING A TASSEL

Cut a rectangular piece of card **1.5cm** ($^1/_2$in) longer than the desired length of the tassel. Wrap thread (usually the stranded cotton used in the cross stitching) around the card lengthways until you have the desired thickness (see fig **6**). Slide the tassel off the card and slip a length of thread through the top of the tassel and tie a knot. Bind the middle or top third of the tassel with another length of thread and finally trim all the threads to the same length.

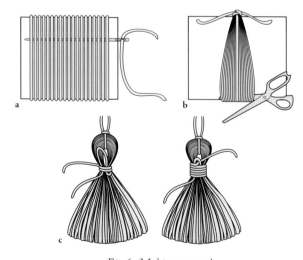

Fig 6 Making a tassel

SUPPLIERS

The Caron Collection
Macleod Craft Marketing, West Yonderton, Warlock
Road, Bridge of Weir, Renfrewshire, PA11 3SR.
Tel: 01505 612618.
*Caron space-dyed threads – Wildflowers, Waterlilies and
Watercolours.*

DMC Creative World
Pullman Road, Wigston, Leicester, LE18 2DY. Tel: 0116
281 1040.
Stranded cotton, Flower thread, Rayon thread, Metallic thread.

Fabric Flair Ltd
Unit 3 Northlands Industrial Estate, Copheap Lane,
Warminster, BA12 0BG. Tel: 01985 846400.
All stitching fabrics and bands, guest towels, Raj Mahal gift box.

Framecraft Miniatures Ltd
372–376 Summer Lane, Hockley, Birmingham, B19 3QA.
Tel: (0121) 2120551.

*Tray, address book, dressing table range, money-box, wooden
bowl, luggage tag, mini bag, booties, quilted glass case, jar lacy,
together with a multitude of other products suitable for displaying
needlework.*

Impress Blank Cards and Craft Materials
Slough Farm, Westhall, Halesworth, Suffolk, IP19 8RN.
Tel: 01986 781422.
Cards and gift tags, digital alarm clock.

Madeira Threads (UK) Ltd
Thirsk Industrial Park, York Road, Thirsk, North
Yorkshire, YO7 3BX. Tel: 01845 524880.
Metallic threads, blending filaments.

The Rainbow Gallery
The Silver Thimble, PO Box 30, Cardiff CF2 7WA.
Rainbow variegated threads (Bravo).

ACKNOWLEDGEMENTS

I would like to thank the following for all their help and support and for being there as friends.
My husband and children who looked after themselves throughout the project with few moans and groans and for
making valuable contributions to the designs when the going got tough!
Dorothy Maynard who worked day and night in order to meet very tight deadlines and whose work is beautiful. Her
calm advice and encouragement have been invaluable especially when I stretched her patience to the limit.
Marina Rees of Quintessential Quilts for making the jewellery roll, toy bag, safari travel pillow, pagoda diary and
cotton wool holder when frantically hectic with work and builders.
Mary Hopkins for sparing very precious time in her very busy life to make up the lovely stitched pieces for the
Borders Galore chapter.
Hilary Nottingham of Kingfisher Gallery for her excellent framing skills not just with the pictures but with awkward
articles such as hair brushes and box lids.
Christmas really sparkles thanks to Sonia for her work in converting scraps of stitching into items of desire.
Rosemary, Clive and staff at Wye Needlecraft, Bakewell, Derbyshire who suggested and supplied me with many of the
threads used. Their mail order service is second to none.
Finally thanks to Cheryl Brown my editor for keeping her cool when tested by designer tantrums!

INDEX

Embroidery

X

9 —

c

Embroidery